"Pastors know that there's no one who understands the particular challenges and joys of ministry better than Craig Barnes. When you read this diary, Craig's delight in, exasperation with, and love for the church is manifest. He's had a privileged look at us from his vantage as pastor, preacher, teacher, and our nation's most prominent seminary president. Has this preacher got a way with words! In this rich collection of some of Craig's best thoughts on the Christian ministry, pastors will find much encouragement and guidance, and anybody else will discover why the pastoral ministry is such a serious, joyful, demanding, and ultimately fulfilling vocation."

—**Will Willimon**, United Methodist Bishop (retired); Duke Divinity School; author of *Accidental Preacher: A Memoir*

"A wise mentor once told me that, apart from a theology of vocation, being a pastor is the best job in the world. In any given week, a pastor is a scholar, author, teacher, counselor, entrepreneur, and manager of a small business. In addition, people invite a pastor into the most sacred, joyful, and intimate spaces and times in life. In this fascinating and beautifully written book, Craig Barnes, employing a creative format, lovingly reveals the challenges and privileged blessings of the pastoral vocation. I found myself nodding in recognition at his insights on the loss of Saturday night, doing a wedding for a nonbeliever, and the Vows section of the Sunday *New York Times* being surprisingly short on traditional church weddings presided over by a pastor. I smiled as well at his description of the Blessed Church Lady and the congregant who, during the greeting after worship, suggested that he find a new barber. Craig Barnes loves being a pastor and finds surprising grace even in ordinary ecclesiastical minutiae. I couldn't put the book down."

—**John M. Buchanan**, former editor and publisher, the *Christian Century*

D1472252

"Craig Barnes offers readers a diary full of grace and truth about pastoral ministry. His writing is a salve for the human soul. But more than that, the Holy haunts this book."

—**Luke A. Powery**, Duke University

"Craig Barnes has more gifts than anyone has a right to have, and many of them shine in *Diary of a Pastor's Soul*: simple and beautiful eloquence, spiritual poignancy and finesse, brilliance in vulnerability, predictability woven in with surprise, and hope that knows the inseparability of sorrow and laughter. The meal Barnes offers us is served up like a harvest of ordinary ruminations from a pastor's soul. It gradually turns out, however, to be more like sitting at Babette's feast, prepared by one specially gifted by God to show us how local and seasonal ingredients of pain, beauty, and faith can be more than enough to reveal a table that is actually laden with truth and grace—for the people and even for the pastor. Take and eat."

—**Mark Labberton**, president, Fuller Theological Seminary

Diary

of a

Pastor's
Soul

THE HOLY MOMENTS
IN A LIFE OF MINISTRY

M. CRAIG BARNES

BrazosPress
a division of Baker Publishing Group
Grand Rapids, Michigan

Published by Brazos Press
a division of Baker Publishing Group
PO Box 6287, Grand Rapids, MI 49516-6287
www.brazospress.com

Printed in the United States of America

This book is a fictionalized telling of the author's life in pastoral ministry. The stories in this diary are not careful depictions of actual events, and the names have been changed to protect the privacy of those involved.

Library of Congress Cataloging-in-Publication Data
Names: Barnes, M. Craig, author.
Title: Diary of a pastor's soul : the holy moments in a life of ministry / M. Craig Barnes.
Description: Grand Rapids, Michigan : Brazos Press, a division of Baker Publishing Group, 2020.
Identifiers: LCCN 2019041771 | ISBN 9781587434440 (paperback)
Subjects: LCSH: Pastoral theology.
Classification: LCC BV4211.3 .B3625 2020 | DDC 253—dc23
LC record available at https://lccn.loc.gov/2019041771

Grateful acknowledgment is made to the *Christian Century* to reprint with permission the following selections: a version of July, week two, "A Faithfully Anonymous Pastor" was previously published in November 22, 2010; a version of September, week four, "Pastoral Lessons from My Sheepdog," was previously published in December 30, 2010; and a version of March, week two, "I Was Done with Words," was previously published in July 13, 2012.

I am grateful to Kathryn Helmers, who is my literary agent, editor of rough drafts, and dear friend since college—a long time ago.

The author is represented by the literary agency of Creative Trust Literary Group, LLC.

20 21 22 23 24 25 26   7 6 5 4 3 2 1

For the Reverend Dr. John Buchanan,
who hired me when I was a hungry graduate student
and has long been my model of a pastor with gravitas

Contents

Contents

Contents

March

April

May

June

Preface

The old Pietists used to write in their journals about *gravitas*. It was their description of a soul that had gained enough weightiness to be attractive, like all things with a gravitational pull. Most people can immediately think about someone in their lives who has this gravitas. Maybe it's a former teacher, coach, grandparent, boss, the woman down the street who happily interrupts her gardening to speak with you, . . . or a really good pastor.

How does the soul of a pastor become well formed in a calling that can just as easily suck it dry as fill it with gravitas? The best way to answer that question is by telling a story and pointing, as if to say "remember that moment when . . ." something holy happened to me. No pastor can pry those moments from God's hand, but an attentive one can behold them. And in the beholding, the pastor's soul is formed.

As I began writing about these moments, I found myself telling stories. That quickly got complicated—not just because I couldn't tell other people's stories without violating pastoral confidentiality but because I found myself wanting to rewrite some of my own stories that I might have lived differently if I had known then what I know now.

At some point I realized there was someone writing alongside me. It was *him*, not me, writing the stories. I had acquired a narrator. It turns out he was reflecting on a life of pastoral ministry by keeping a weekly diary in the final year preceding his retirement from his long service to his congregation. So many of his experiences appeared ordinary—when actually they were moments of holy formation for his soul.

When I gathered these diary entries for publication, the question immediately came up whether this was a book of fiction or nonfiction. It's not a novel, but neither is it didactic. After all, a pastor with gravitas learns to leave behind the need to work in neat categories. The formation of the pastoral soul does not lend itself to being explained as much as revealed, by beholding "that moment when . . ." So I hope that younger pastors, of all genders, will find these reflections helpful as they inevitably journey through similar experiences in their congregations.

I wish my life and ministry had been conducted as reflectively as the pastor who wrote this diary. I'm not the man revealed through the details of these ruminations, but much of the writing is a fictionalized depiction of my experiences after thirty-seven years of pastoral ministry.

What most pastors are thinking about as they drive home from their retirement party is not how excited they are to be free of working for the church. They're thinking that it all went pretty fast, cost so much more than they could have anticipated, and profoundly changed them along the way. And they're reassuring themselves that they made a difference with this use of their lives.

What are the parishioners thinking as they leave that retirement party? Some are thinking the pastor stayed too long. Others are already making plans for the next one to arrive. But most are just grateful. Their gratitude is not just for all the programs, hospital visits, weddings, funerals, growth in the membership, or faithful trips to the pulpit with carefully crafted sermons. The attentive parishioners are grateful for the glimpses they received into their pastor's soul. That's the only important thing a servant of the church brings to the ministry. The rest is just necessary skills that are learned, and very hard work that is inevitable if the job is to be done well.

Typically, people with gravitas are older, but it really has less to do with their age than with their response to the way life unfolds. They have scars, which are strangely attractive, but not open wounds. They've settled into themselves, and into the people God has given them to love, without any irritating plans for improvement. But they remain curious about the most ordinary things they find in those they care about. People with gravitas have discovered that the Holy haunts the landscape of life, and they gently probe every glimpse they find, whether it's buried in the ordinary, the fleeting moments of delight and surprise, or the places of pain, as it often is.

No one is born with gravitas, and it's not exactly a spiritual gift. It comes as a result of good responses to hurts, blessings, failures, achievement, boredom, and obligations, all of which are surrendered to our Creator. Some who have the exact same experiences turn instead to cynicism. But souls with gravitas somehow choose to receive their lives, such as they are, with gratitude.

M. Craig Barnes

I pray I've done so...

Prologue

BY THE DIARIST

I've never been the kind of person who keeps a diary. Never even tried before tonight. But I now find myself irresistibly drawn to the idea.

My wife Ellie and I have decided that one year from now, I will retire as the senior pastor of St. Andrews Presbyterian Church. Since last Christmas we've talked about it off and on, but never with a sense of commitment to the idea. Somehow this spring we crossed over into a realization that the time had come.

I'll turn sixty-eight in a month, and Ellie is a few years behind me, which means if we want to have a retirement, we'd better get on with it. This will be the twenty-eighth anniversary of my installation service as the pastor of St. Andrews, and the forty-third anniversary of my ordination. I like the idea of leaving before we hit any more round numbers that need celebrating. No one at the church has indicated—at least not to me—that it's high time for me to move on. Some of that came up after I first arrived, but long ago the congregation and I settled into each other.

Neither Ellie nor I are sure how I will handle retiring. She took early retirement years ago from her career as a social worker. She's never regretted it. But we both have doubts about me apart from St. Andrews. We have no plan other than feeling like we need to leave town to make plenty of room for the new pastor. After making the last tuition payment for our daughter Mackenzie, we bought a cabin on a lake that has long been our vacation home. I suppose we'll settle in there until it's time for the Old Presbyterian Pastors Retirement Home. I'm a little worried about what lies ahead, but I would really like to use this year to think carefully about what I'm leaving behind.

St. Andrews and I have had highs and lows over the years, and a lot of long stretches that were not particularly high or low. It was in the ordinariness of parish life that I found myself deeply committed to the congregation. There was always another funeral and another baptism, another associate pastor coming and going, another Advent and Easter, and so very many weekly sermons along the way that were neither brilliant nor dull but hopefully faithful to the gospel. There were also moments of crisis, like when the steeple caught fire after a lightning strike, and moments of joy like we'll hopefully have when the construction on the new Christian education wing is completed next year. But pastors easily rise to crises and joys. The challenge is to pay attention to the ordinary rhythms, the daily manna, and find the traces of divine grace.

I was never keeping count of it all. But now that I know this is going to be my last year, I feel the need to pay more attention to what I hope will be another ordinary year of pastoral ministry. And if there are surprises, I'll search for the grace in that as well. Thus, this diary. I'll try to write a page or two every week, always searching for the sacred subtext of what's been unfolding beneath the surface of my ministry all these years. As I now understand, that's where I keep finding the Savior at work.

July

Writing the Faith in Stone

It looks like we've finally found a way to get Alice Matthews off the property committee. She's ruled it for twenty-three years. All the decisions about how we would use the church's facilities, including the sanctuary, have had to pass through the committee she's run with an iron will to maintain the church's heritage—or at least her vision of it. When I speak about ministry, her eyes always glaze over.

Alice has always focused on our gray stone church building: its beautiful oak doors, the parlor that the women's association keeps redecorating, the spire in constant need of repair. It's not a particularly large church. The sanctuary can comfortably seat six hundred people, which we see only on Christmas Eve and Easter. Alice refers to the architecture as neo-Gothic. My wife Ellie refers to it as Gothic-wannabe.

If it weren't for Alice's inability to continue driving at night, I doubt we would have been able to pull off retiring her from her service/domain on the property committee. This evening we concluded the meeting with a little cake and coffee to thank her for her long service as its chair. I said some appreciative words to this woman with whom I have constantly sparred for over two decades.

Alice doesn't hate me, love me, or even think much about me as her pastor. In her mind I am always just the next necessary person in a robe for her church. After all, churches have to have a pastor, she understands. She typically sits through worship, but I never get a sense that she is engaged either by the liturgy or by the sermon I spent so many hours constructing. For Alice, I'm pretty much beside the point.

She never actually had to say, "I was here before you and will still be here after you." We both knew it was true. But the problem of aging caught up with her, finally moving her out of power. This is the pastor's last great hope for conflicts with old parishioners.

Much of the current literature on ministry indicates that people like Alice Matthews are exactly the problem with the church today. Some even claim that she's the person who is whittling away at the souls of pastors who are knocking themselves out to inflame their congregations with passion for the mission of Christ.

But now that she is out of the way, I'm already wondering if there is not something more to her soul than I saw.

She's part of a generation that believed in institutions and their buildings. Sturdy things you can count on. They're not going to be easily discarded because a pastor comes back from a conference with a new laminated notebook filled with the latest ideas for church renewal. It doesn't matter how awful the new soprano is in the choir, or how bad the sermon, you can still get a blessing by just walking up the old wooden stairs to the balcony whose creaks and moans echo the aches and pains of all the saints before us who trudged up those stairs after a hard week's work.

Alice is an anti-Gnostic. She likes to find her holiness in the dust and gritty realities of the church building and all the memories they hold. While the services seem to do little for her, just being in the building allows her soul to exhale. It was within these walls that she was married, her children were baptized, her daughter married, and her husband's funeral was conducted. Everything she knows about Jesus and his grace for us is lingering in the mortar that holds the stones of her church together.

It's not that she's against ministry and mission as much as she is for the physical church itself. If my new program for opening the church gym to neighborhood kids means they might spill something on the floor or, God forbid, smoke pot in the bathroom, she will throw her shriveled body across the doors. But if I take up an offering for a program to help children in Haiti, she will dig deep in her purse.

She says she understands the need for "all these mission projects." And I think she really does care about the poor. But our primary mission in The Gospel According to Alice is caretaking our temple. She and I have very different understandings of the church, and over the years we just kept bumping up against that fundamental disagreement, especially when it came to the church budget.

I keep preaching, literally, that we cannot participate in the mission of Christ that sends us to Jerusalem, Judea, Samaria, and the ends of the earth and keep our hearts inside the temple. This is one of the first lessons the early church had to learn. I know that I'm right and that Alice is as wrong as she can be about our congregation's priority.

But I also know that for over two thousand years the church has never fully left its affection for a temple of holiness. This is why we used to spend all our money building cathedrals that took centuries to construct. We were looking for a glimpse of dwelling in the Holy. Some of us still are. When I'm a guest preacher at a booming new church meeting in a facility whose architect is probably also responsible for the Best Buy stores, the walls don't suggest that our faith is sturdy. Or that someone was here before us. Or that we are here to behold the beauty of the Lord.

So how do we follow the mission of Christ to go into all the world if we are lugging these heavy Gothic buildings on our back?

And how do we follow Christ's call to leave all and follow him without sacrificing the stained-glass windows with the weathered brass plaque tacked on the bottom that says "In Memory of . . ."? It's as if the little plaque is whispering, "Don't forget me as you forge ahead into your new ever-so-relevant ministry, or you will also forget who you have always been."

I think we may be losing something core to our faith in moving Alice Matthews out of the way of the church's progress. Of course, she had to go. The mission is the mission, and our faith has never survived by being a comfortable place of memories. I get that. But I wonder what it does to our souls to so easily forget things like place and the holy memories that are attached to them.

A Faithfully Anonymous Pastor

Once a year I teach a class on pastoral ministry at our local seminary. Although it adds a lot of work, I keep saying yes to the invitation because I really love working with the students. Most of them impress me with their dedication to Jesus Christ and the pastoral ministry. Occasionally I encounter a student like Brad Landis who renews my hope in the future of the church.

He's almost thirty years old, rustically handsome, and one of the smartest students I can remember. But he hides his brilliance beneath a bushel of deferring shyness. In the few times he spoke up in my class, he always began by clearing his throat and pushing his horn-rimmed glasses back up on his nose, as if he were imitating Clark Kent. Then he would suggest a profound insight from our theological tradition.

Brad finished seminary in May at the head of his class and could have gone on to graduate school to earn a PhD. Several of the other professors, including the dean, confronted him with his amazing gifts for scholarship. I did the same once after class. "To whom much is given, much is required," I tried. He nodded deferentially. But he was always clear on his calling and wanted only to serve a local congregation—preferably a small one.

He said yes to the first church that offered him a job. Last Sunday I preached at the worship service where he was ordained and installed as the pastor of a rural congregation in Michigan. From the airport it took me two hours of country driving, and getting lost more than once, to find the church address that MapQuest had overlooked.

Once the ordination worship service began, I looked out at the congregation of worried farmers, worn-out homemakers, and bored teenagers. A yellowed fluorescent light hummed its way through the whole service. The microphone on the pulpit squealed if you got too close. The floor fans moaned as they vainly tried to cool the summer heat. Even the laments of the building were part of this sacred conversation between congregation, God, and the new pastor. It occurred to me that I had never written an exam as challenging as the one he would face every Sunday.

Karl Barth claimed that his early years as the pastor of a blue-collar congregation in Safenwil were formative for the insights that led to his major theological breakthroughs as a professor. But as I sat in that chancel and watched my former student kneel to accept the laying on of hands, I wondered how many brilliant Karl Barths there have been who never left their Safenwil.

My former student has no strategic plan for "turning this church around." Brad's only ambition is to be the next in a long line of faithfully anonymous pastors who never move on to prestigious positions. But he isn't anonymous to these people who know his name.

He'll spend his years baptizing their babies, helping to deliver a calf in the middle of the night, serving on the school board, burying husbands who died too soon, attending Fourth of July picnics, negotiating debates about how to pay for the new church roof—and then every Sunday he will stand in their pulpit and make holy sense of it all.

When the ordination service was over, we all made our way to the basement fellowship hall for a potluck dinner. Tables perched over beige linoleum were adorned with red-and-white-checked vinyl cloths and small, handmade arrangements of daisies. Families and friends plopped into the gray metal folding chairs as they ate, laughed, gossiped, and teased. Several women fussed over the serving tables filled with casseroles, salads, overly fried chicken, and jello with slices of pears trapped inside. Children squealed as they chased each other around the room. I overheard a story about summer being a great time to get a good deal on snow tires.

They could have been discussing their anxieties about the future of family farms, the economy, or "just where is this country heading?" But there was none of that today. Even the small talk had a lilt to it.

I understood why when their new pastor entered the room and I saw how many of his parishioners just wanted to touch him. Brad never even made it to a chair. One after another they got up from the tables wiping their hands in order to shake his, or give him a hug, or pat him on the back. One man had tears in his eyes.

This was a Eucharistic feast. A new pastor had come, and the congregation took it as a sign that God knew how to find them. The holiness of the room became so apparent I almost took off my shoes. No one wanted to leave, certainly not me. Least of all, the new pastor.

This was my glimpse into a mystery about the mainline church that is hidden from all the statistics and anxiety about its decline. I have no idea what hardships lie ahead for this congregation, or even how long it will last. But I do know that today they are filled with expectancy. In their midst is another highly capable pastor who is prepared to bring thousands of years of theological hope to bear on a community—one that finds holiness by sitting in a church basement swapping stories about the new snow tire that is sure to get you through the winter that always comes for us.

The Pastor's Wife and the Mustang

Tomorrow is our wedding anniversary and I still don't have a present. I've never been good at this. When I was younger I thought something as simple as buying an anniversary gift shouldn't be so hard. Now I've settled into not knowing what Ellie wants. I actually love that about her.

There is a mystery about this woman that sometimes drives me crazy, but mostly makes me want to keep asking her out on a first date.

Before we were married, she was candid about the costly mistakes she had made in her early twenties, and said she had decided it was time to start taking her life, and her faith, more seriously. I remember being impressed by her resolve and envious of her mistakes. By the time I met her, she had made so many healthy choices and was now well respected, but that persevering, irrepressible streak of something inappropriate in her fascinated me. Once while visiting her apartment I walked in while she was trying to assemble an IKEA desk. When I came through the door a screwdriver sailed across the room as she screamed, "*Mother*——*!*" That may have been the moment I decided to ask her to marry me.

Now that our years together have piled up, I've become accustomed to living with two very different women in this marriage. In addition to the cleaned-up, respectable pastor's wife she wants to be, the wild woman who frightens her was also at the altar when we exchanged vows.

That wild woman will not be ignored, is not ever going to leave, nor will she allow me to consume her with understanding. I can't avoid flirting with her, but she's way out of my league, and we both know it. And the last thing she ever wants to hear when she's disappointed, which is often, is something that sounds pastoral.

The woman Ellie prefers to be takes pride in her pies, buys Christmas presents for the church staff while we're on summer vacation, says kind things about my sermon even when we both know it didn't quite work that morning, and always sits at the end of the third pew, left side. The untamed woman hides through most of that.

Both women raised our daughter Mackenzie. There's a photo on the dresser of our bedroom with her leaning over an infant, cooing. It's a glimpse of total delight. Unlike me, Ellie never missed a soccer game, piano recital, or ballet performance. She went to Barnes & Noble to get books on algebra so that she could help with homework, and later with SAT exams. I often came home from an evening committee meeting at church to find the two of them lying on our bed, sometimes talking about a boy, sometimes in a tickling contest. But when Mackenzie went through the classic stage of adolescent rebellion, she knew her mother was a lioness who didn't mind eating her young. It helped with the boundaries issue.

Ellie spent most of her career as a social worker employed by an adoption agency before burning out and taking early retirement. Her job was to be the advocate for birth mothers who decided to give up their babies for adoption. She would help them review the applications, in which couples described why they would be great adoptive parents, and then make a choice. Sometimes the birth mother changed her mind after the baby was already placed in a home. Then it was Ellie's job to drive to the adoptive parents' house and take the baby out of their arms. She left a bit of her heart with each of those weeping couples, and eventually too much of her heart for doing social good was gone. She became a part-time interior designer. She said it was easier to fix living rooms than lives. But she has lots of other projects.

Tonight she's out in the garage working on her rusted-out 1967 Mustang. Again. She inherited the car a few years ago from her crazy uncle who adored her. She was startled that this was his bequest to her when he died. And then delighted. "This car is a classic!" she kept telling me. So we towed it back to our house, because it didn't run, and now it has settled into our garage, forcing us to park our working cars along the curb.

She knew nothing about cars before diving into this renovation project—shortly after she burned out on fixing up people. Since then she's spent countless hours on YouTube and talking to her now-good-friend Ray at the counter of the local auto parts dealer, trying to figure out what it will take to finally restore the old classic. I keep finding new tools on the kitchen table. And I love it when she strolls into the study at home with grease on another one of my old T-shirts.

She keeps telling me this car was meant to be flaunted on the street. But I wonder which old Mustang we're really talking about.

Week Four

Pastoral Care as Déjà Vu

Jenny Adams came in today to talk again about how much she doesn't like her job at the bank, and to ask for the third time what she should do. I shrugged and said, "I dunno." (This is when people figure out why pastoral counseling is free.) Then I tried telling her she was free to quit if she wanted, but she shouldn't expect the next job to make her any happier.

She looked crestfallen. She insists on thinking that a job can make her feel fulfilled, and she is not impressed when I tell her it's just a job and it can't save her.

I was tempted this morning to say, "Look, Jenny. We've been here before. You're going to tell me how unhappy you are in your work. I'm going to tell you, again, that you're free to quit. You're not going to do that because by now you've realized that Shangri La isn't hiring, but you need a job. I'll offer the nicest prayer I can come up with, and you'll leave thanking me for my time. And nothing will change. Let's just save ourselves the hour and cut to the end of the conversation." But, of course, I didn't say anything like that. I just listened, again, biting my finger. I've done that so many times I think I may have some nerve damage in it.

When I began my job as a pastor, like Jenny I had so much expectation and ambition for my work. In those days I wanted to do something spectacular with my life that would impress God. But that was a long time ago. Now I realize anything I accomplished that was remotely helpful was all grace. Every great idea I had could have driven the church into a ditch, and more than one of them did. Even when my plans worked out, God was still not all that impressed.

God seems to prefer the ordinary and routine. Most of creation was designed to be held together by repetition, the same things happening again and again, whether it's little things like electrons spinning around in circles, or huge things like planets slowly revolving around the sun every year. Winter, spring, summer, fall. Praise God from whom all blessings flow.

My devotions this morning came from Philippians 4, where the apostle Paul says, "Finally, beloved, whatever is true, whatever is honorable, whatever is just, whatever is pure, whatever is pleasing, whatever is commendable . . . keep on doing those things." Apparently, he learned that God is mostly impressed by routine acts of faithfulness.

These were perhaps the last written words of a man whose ambition was to plant congregations all over the Roman Empire. But without any rational reason to believe that the church would actually succeed, he ends his life by telling us just to do whatever is right. "Keep on doing" it, he says. Do it again and again. "And the God of peace will be with you." He might as well have said to keep listening to Jenny Adams tell you how unfulfilled she is at work, but listen as her pastor who can offer her better concerns for her life.

Most of ministry is just doing small things as faithfully as possible—getting to the next committee meeting, burying people with dignity and placing them back into the hands of God, trying to talk the church treasurer into signing a check for a new copier, that's not in the budget, officiating at weddings when you're worried about this new marriage, figuring out what to do with the custodian who's become surly, and of course having something to say on Sunday that sounds like a Word from the Lord. And keep on listening to parishioners who lament their relationships and jobs but aren't going to make changes because they've settled into a lifestyle they don't really like. Pastoral ministry involves a lot of déjà vu all over again.

The challenge is not to rise above the ordinary routines but to find the holiness in them. This has always been one of the reasons people need pastors—to help them behold the quiet miracle of having the God of peace with us.

Now if I could just get Jenny to be as concerned about her prayer life as she is her job, she may find some of that peace. Then she would be free to get on with her mission of being a Christian in this very messed-up world. That would be impressive.

It may happen. While I've learned the importance of ordinary and routine acts of faithfulness, I've also had to enhance my capacity for surprises. People like Jenny Adams actually do change their lives sometimes, and congregations do take heroic risks, and cities do revitalize. And to all who will listen I will constantly invite them to the freedom they have to make these changes. But as a pastor my calling is not to love my dreams for them more than I love them as they are today. So I keep on doing what love requires, again and again, while waiting for Jesus to do what only he can: change people.

Few things are more dangerous for pastors than expectations. This is not only because they set us up for disappointment but also because they are actually veiled attempts at controlling the future. Congregations are not easily controlled, nor should they be. They belong to God, and who can know the plans of the Holy for their future?

Rather than expectations, I've learned to maintain expectancy, which is a sense of awe at the divine-human encounter that is breaking in on everything we call ordinary and routine. The encounter is not always apparent, which is another reason why Jenny needs a pastor who can help her see the sacred subtext to her life. I'll be ready for her next appointment, and I'll wait for the one when she comes to tell me it was never about her job.

August

Week One

Saying "I Love You"

Today was the last Sunday before heading out for vacation. No one in the parish begrudges me this time of renewal. They all get breaks from their own hard work and think of vacation as an entitlement. I think of it as a swimmer who dives down too deep and has to break the surface to breathe again.

As a sign of being "off," I always stop shaving on vacation. This summer I began the practice a couple of weeks early. Our older parishioners are not impressed, and they think I've taken off work a bit early. As she left the worship service this morning, old Mrs. Johnson leaned up on her four-footed cane to say, "I hope if I die while you're gone you'll shave off that awful summer beard before coming back to conduct my funeral."

Most people pleasantly asked about our vacation plans, even though they know we'll go back to the same cabin by the lake we've owned for years. And this summer we're also looking forward to a trip to Scotland. But maybe there is something more in the polite question. Maybe even Mrs. Johnson was trying to say, "I'll miss my pastor while you're away getting air back in your soul."

Every time I leave on vacation, I say "I love you" as part of the benediction. The words are true because I will be away from those who long ago settled into my heart. Even while enjoying a cigar on the cabin porch and the next Marilynne Robinson novel, I will fret inappropriately about the fall officers retreat that is far from put together, or appropriately about Mrs. Johnson, who really could die before I can get back to place the sign of the cross on her forehead. She's a battle-axe, but she's our battle-axe, and I just love her. Of course I'll shave to do her funeral.

Others of the congregation who walked past me following worship this morning took their time to shake my hand and say, "We love you too." It seems to them like the right, risky thing to say. How else could they respond to my vulnerability in the benediction? I think they know we are fumbling around trying to describe our relationship that somehow involves love, even though the relationship is so uneven—me being their pastor and all that entails.

It's awkward, clumsy even, to tell a congregation that you're in love with them. After all these years of trying to say this, I still feel like a junior high school boy passing a note to a girl that says, "I really, really like you."

I used to think it would be easier to love the congregation at the end of vacation when I was full of air again. But it is actually when I am depleted and more than a little grumpy that I find my heart is most caught up with being their pastor. Even my worst arguments with the church last year were old lovers' quarrels. Their addicted hand-wringing makes my eyes roll, unfortunately often in committee meetings, and my next unrealistic idea makes them sigh and essentially say, "Really?" But we've figured out long ago that we belong together.

At least these are the reassurances I give myself as I leave the depths and head back to the surface for a bit.

A Sunday with the *New York Times*

Last week I began vacation, which meant I didn't have to fret on Saturday night about a sermon that still wasn't working. It also meant that I could leisurely make my way through the *New York Times* on Sunday morning. I love that treat. Ellie and I usually still get to the nearby church for worship, at her insistence, but when the hour is over I tuck back in to my seclusion at our cabin with the *NYT*. I know I can get it online, but I love the feel, smell, and smeared ink of the real newspaper.

I even read The Vows section of the paper, which described the weddings of twenty-three couples. It was striking to me how rare it was to find a couple married in a church by a pastor. Most of them were married by something like the Marriage Bureau or a cousin who took the trouble of getting ordained on the internet for the sake of helping out at the wedding that was held in a hotel, the park, or an old barn that had been converted into a chapel. Far more important to the reporter, there was usually a nearby white tent for the elegant reception. The church now has little to do with most weddings.

I don't actually regret this as much as I'm supposed to. I no longer feel a need to protect the church's turf as a place where weddings must be conducted. Over the years I have knocked myself out to smuggle something sacred into the lavish ceremonies in our sanctuary that were always going to be about the bride's dreams, the confused little ring bearer or flower girl, the hungover groomsmen, and the bridesmaids who were grumpy that their dresses didn't fit. If the secular world really wants to take over the weddings, I grouse, it can have them.

But then I ponder what was going on in the hearts of the bride and groom when they recited the ever-so-personal vows they wrote for this critical moment in their lives. They probably weren't thinking it was just another detail before getting to the white tent, the overcooked salmon, or the paper napkins monogrammed with their initials. They were hoping this was their moment for a dream to come true. When they said something at least similar to "I promise to always be your spouse," they actually meant it. And with those simple words they threw their lives together with no idea about the devastating costs and unimaginable delights it would create. In my old age, I find myself wondering if maybe this is still religious even though the naïve couple has no idea of it being so.

Even the *NYT* has enough respect for the holiness of this moment to label the wedding section "The Vows." To make a vow is to create a covenant, not a contract. Our society is weary of contracts that tediously depict what you have to do in order for me to do what you want, but we all yearn for a covenant with someone who will say, "I'll love you no matter what."

When a couple says that, whether or not they realize it, they are reaching up to heaven. That's because there is no human way anyone can possibly fulfill such a vow.

Even if people have wandered away from church with no intention of returning, the prodigals discover that the memory of the Father's house still returns to them. That's never more true than when they are trying to weave their flawed lives into each other. God knows, there is no reason to have any hope that this vow will endure given all their other promises that have not. After so many years of premarital counseling, I've come to realize there's usually plenty of anxiety in the couple as they worry about that too.

Hopefully the church will be there for these couples should they figure out it is time to leave behind the field of daisies and come into a house of worship. Maybe that will happen after another horrible fight and they are out of energy for any more. Or when they discover what "in sickness and in health" actually means. Or maybe they will become interested in God when they have children, who will expose the limits of their capacity to be always loving.

Somehow the day will come, I am sure, when they need a house of worship. What I do not know is if they realize this is what they need, or even that the church will know how to receive them should they wander in with their tattered vows.

In-Laws and the Priest Thing

We just returned from Ellie's family reunion. These things happen about every two years, and that's about the right amount of time. They clearly love each other, and the embraces at the beginning and end of the weekend are authentic, but it doesn't take long for the complexity of their histories with each other to emerge. They may as well be wearing nametags scrawled with too much truth like, "Sister who was always Daddy's favorite."

I like being the Gentile-in-law at these events, and the guy Ellie uses late at night to figure out what she should say to her brother whose daughter isn't speaking to him after his divorce. My own family of origin is plenty dysfunctional, and I don't need to take responsibility for another one. But I've grown very fond of her family, always as the Gentile.

They're Irish Catholic, so it's difficult for everyone in the family to figure out what to do with the Protestant pastor (priest?) who joined their family long ago. Since they're all lapsed Catholics it was devastating only for their mother, the last of them to take Mass seriously, when I married one of the daughters of the family. She got over that when Mackenzie was born, and at her funeral the family asked me to give one of the eulogies. All of them have been only gracious to me, but "The Priest Thing" is what's always scrawled on my nametag at these family reunions.

All of Ellie's siblings have done very well professionally and, like me, are now contemplating retirement. They have a lot more money than we do, and their kids are making kids of their own. Although none of them are particularly devoted to the church, they're neither impressed nor worried that Ellie brought a pastor into the family. They just never knew what to make of it.

Early on, they used to watch their language around me or apologize about an off-color joke, or if the conversations were starting to run out of topics, they'd ask me questions about the pope. But long ago they realized that I'm not just the pastor who has come over for a polite dinner, and since I'm going to be hanging around, they should just get back to their normal reactive relationships with each other.

The "priest thing" still confuses them, however, and they can't figure out what I do for a living or why I do it. They think of it as something somehow holy, and therefore confusing and distancing, but probably important. And they're not at all clear about how the wild sister ended up marrying someone they assumed was already married to God.

I've faced the same clumsiness when sitting next to someone on an airplane, or on the bleachers of my daughter's many soccer games, or at a fundraising dinner for a community organization. As soon as someone asks me, "And what do you do for a living?" I know what every pastor knows—the conversation is about to take a turn around an awkward corner. After saying, "I'm a pastor," I sometimes hear about their bad experience with the church. At other times, if they press further to learn that I'm a Presbyterian pastor, they'll start trying to convert me to becoming a real Christian. Most of the time people just nod as they say, "Oh." Then comes the long pause. And then comes the fumbling effort to pretend that didn't just happen, and we surely have something else to talk about. But they're going to keep their eye on me.

Even my own parishioners keep me at just a bit of a distance. And yet they make appointments to come and tell me the most intimate things about their lives. I've learned why Catholics prefer to have a screen in front of the priest when they enter a confessional. It's the anonymity and confidentiality that make it work. When they see me in the church's fellowship hall they are pretty certain I'm not trading their secrets with others in the congregation. But the fact that I know their secrets is the screen between us in any public setting. I might as well work for the IRS. You know it's necessary, but you don't want to get too close.

The reality is that we all have the same secrets. We were judged by our parents when we were children, and by our children when they became adults. We were judged by our teachers, coaches, bosses, neighbors, and more severely by our spouses. But worst of all was the judgment by the same person who keeps showing up in the bathroom mirror to say, "Not nearly good enough." None of us can believe what we've done and left undone. Is this really a secret?

But no one who has just become aware that she or he is sitting next to someone who has spent time in a confessional, which we Protestants call pastoral counseling, is ever going to fully relax. I'm not actually trying to talk to God about their lives while we sit on the bleachers, but that's what they're worried about. I don't even talk to God about my own life as much as I should.

I got used to this clumsy dynamic a long time ago, and it doesn't really bother me anymore. More than one therapist has suggested that it's my own introverted nature that makes me comfortable with the little distance it creates. But I don't think that's right. Or at least it's not exactly right. It's also the cost of wearing the priest nametag.

When I try to explain this odd dynamic to our interns, or the students at the local seminary, they argue that it's an outdated mode of professionalism that has no place in our more egalitarian understanding of ministry today. But when the pastors who've been at work for even a few years get together at a conference that was supposed to be about some new program for congregational revitalization, they usually find each other in a coffee shop or hotel bar just because they want to sit in a circle with a few other people who understand the cost. The greatest cost is not the crummy salaries, or the mean parishioner who's in every congregation, or even the relentless return of Sundays. It's the nametag.

This doesn't make pastors special. Whenever there's a family reunion, as with every Sunday morning, everyone has to wear some tag that says something about them. And it doesn't matter how wonderful the sermon or music of worship may be: after the coffee hour, most people leave church thinking that's about all they can take. But they're family. So they'll be back.

Week Four

The Blessing of Old Faith

Ellie and I concluded our vacation with a ten-day trip to Scotland, which was beyond wonderful. When Sunday came, I again tried to tell her that every day of vacation is a sabbath. But she again pressed our need to worship with a community of faith on Sunday mornings. We went to the small local Church of Scotland for their 11:00 service.

We were surprised to discover that the congregation was remembering its twelve hundredth anniversary that day. As impressive as that number was to us, we were even more impressed that the members of the church were only sort of impressed. There were no banners, parties, visiting dignitaries, or announcement of a new capital campaign. The congregation was just quietly acknowledging that they had been worshiping in this location for a very long time, and they were thanking God for the divine providence that had been with them all these long years. Most of that acknowledgment came from their session clerk, who read a brief summary of the congregation's history. The pastor's sermon was her next installment from a series on Job.

It was as if they were saying, "Yes, of course. This sounds like the gospel to us. It perseveres through the highs and lows of

44

kings and queens, famines, wars, modernity, and whatever else history brought to the church. Or even what the church has done to itself. The gospel is still here. Now, back to today's text from Scripture."

I am still brooding over what it would mean to live out a tradition so integral to one's identity that you occasionally give thanks for it all the while thinking, "Of course."

Perhaps an American analogy is the annual Thanksgiving dinner. A family that has a history of love and hurt gathers at a table to essentially say, "Yup, this is our family." There are no Thanksgiving parties, presents, or carols. There is typically at least some level of family stress, and it's probably going to show up at the meal, but that's the liturgy the family has repeated for years. Still, it is easier to find equilibrium in a flawed family than in the illusion that we can survive for long as prodigals with no memory of home.

Far more profound than this is the celebration of Holy Communion. No one is ever surprised by the sacrament. We're not supposed to be. As hard as this is for most Americans today, if we could see that our marred congregational family has been coming to the Lord's Table for two thousand years, we would see that the strength of the gathering is found in its modesty, which quietly proclaims, "Remember, this is us. We're a people who need a Savior." But we may, even if only in fleeting moments, also see the overwhelming comfort of such rehearsed identity.

When the winds are blowing hard and the branches are falling, it helps to know that this is not the first storm and that the family tree is deeply rooted.

A day after we returned from Scotland, I went through the pile of mail left on our kitchen table by the house sitter. Among the pile was a form letter from a seminary classmate who is serving a church in California. He included the brochure advertising all the events celebrating his congregation's twenty-fifth anniversary.

Every church anniversary deserves a celebration, I suppose. But it's particularly important for those of us serving younger congregations in this country to keep telling the faith stories of the old congregations as if they were our stories, which of course they are.

September

Pastor, Not Friend

Year after year, the rhythm remains the same. Go away for a summer break to recover who I am, and then slowly give that renewal away to the congregation. It doesn't feel like a sacrifice, and by the end of vacation I'm always eager to get back to work. But halfway through the year, Ellie will talk about how much she misses the guy who was hanging out at the cabin with her last August.

The first big event of every fall is the annual officers retreat, which we just finished. It really isn't a retreat as much as a planning meeting for the year ahead. But we like the idea of putting this in the context of a spiritual retreat. There's a devotional, a prayer, and then we hit the calendar hard for most of our hours together. I doubt Jesus had the same strategy with his disciples, but this is one of the ways Presbyterians love God—we organize things.

The elders of St. Andrews are the people I know best and love deepest. Most of them. I've worked with them in countless committee meetings and have stood beside them through the inevitable conflicts that accompany our attempts to lead the church. I have prayed over their hospital beds, married off their kids, buried their spouses, and baptized their grandchildren. They're dear to me, as I know I am to them. But we're not exactly friends. Or at least that's not the reason the church hired me. I was hired to be the pastor. And it's critical that I remain clear about that in our relationships.

One of the elders made her way to the officers retreat carrying a lukewarm latte from Starbucks. Three years ago she called me in the middle of the night after her son shot himself in the head. Her faith these days is as lukewarm as the coffee, and she misses the days when belief was easy. Another elder at the table was a man who's long enjoyed a reputation in the congregation as a successful businessman and who's trusted to be the chair of the finance committee, but only I know that he's filed for bankruptcy. And then there was the chair of the Christian education committee, who is still furious with me because last year I fired the director of Christian education.

I love these people because I find Christ at work in every dark, protected closet of their hearts, which they readily reveal to me as their pastor. I have even learned how to respond to the call to love those who pretty consistently oppose my leadership. That's because my calling is to serve them. And they are very clear about that.

If any member of the church were in the hospital, and one of the deacons visited before I did, it wouldn't matter if that deacon had just prayed the paint off the walls. At the end of the visit the person in the bed would ask, "When is the pastor coming to see me?" That's not because I'm the best pray-er in the congregation, which I'm not. It's because I took a vow to hold the congregation in my soul, and they will hold me to that devotion.

Peter Tembroke helped organize the officers retreat because he's taken over as the clerk of session since Mrs. Parker had to give up the job. He's an attorney who helped me buy and sell a couple of houses, has seen all my tax returns, and wrote my will. He knows everything about my finances. A couple of times a month we play racquetball. I officiated at his daughter's wedding and sat beside him when he was trying to bail her new husband out of jail after a DUI. We are beyond vulnerable with each other. I know that in any church conflict Peter will always choose to stand beside me even if he's unclear of my position. That sure sounds like friendship, but it can't be. I still owe it to Peter to remember that I'm first and foremost his pastor. That doesn't place me above him, but it places me as one who is always ready to serve his life with God.

Another elder at St. Andrews is an orthopedic surgeon. When I ruptured my Achilles tendon ten years ago, I went to him for treatment. He immediately said I needed surgery. I asked if we could talk about other treatments. He laughed and said, "This isn't a church committee meeting." As friendly as the surgeon and I have always been, our relationship in his office was not one of mutuality. The only way he could heal me was by insisting on his role as my trained physician. When that surgeon later came into my office to tell me his marriage was breaking up, we didn't have a committee meeting then either. He needed me to know how to help him handle his broken heart.

Since hardworking pastors devote most of their energy to the church, they inevitably become close to the lay leaders who work hard beside them. After a long committee meeting or Bible study an elder always lingers at the table with me to talk about our life issues. We always start with their concerns, but the caring elder will always ask, "And how are you doing?" Over the years we've become deeply invested in the anxieties each of us has about our children or the worrisome lab report received from the doctor. We've laughed at each other as we clumsily rebuilt a roof on a mission trip. And we've had so many lunches together. All this makes us close, but not friends.

When I knelt to receive the laying on of hands for my ordination, the elders of the congregation had an unconscious reflex to push me away with those hands. Just a little bit. They were essentially saying, "We are setting you apart to serve us. You can't be just one of the gang anymore. Hopefully you can be friendly, but never again a friend. Now you have to love us enough to no longer expect mutuality because you have to be the pastor. In fact, it's not enough for you to maintain the spiritual disciplines, stay in good communication with Jesus, and even take an August vacation for the sake of your own soul; you've got to have a healthy soul for our sake." It wasn't long after I stood up from the ordination prayer that I discovered this reality. The tricky part is that most church members will say the pastor is of course a dear friend, but in fact they will never let that happen. And shouldn't.

Pure friendships enjoy mutuality. If the elders and I had a completely mutual relationship, it would mean that I am free to say, "You know some days I wonder if there is a God." But no one wants to hear that from a pastor. Since I'm clear about my call to nurture faith in the parish, I can never tell them the hard truths about how low my own search for this faith can travel. That's not why they pay me. People don't pay for their friends. As soon as I cashed my first check from the church I was essentially accepting the role of being a hired hand—ideally one who is cherished, but still a servant with a mortgage who is clear about his ordination vows.

This is what pastors really mean when they talk about the loneliness of their ministry. The irony is that pastors are surrounded by more people than anyone in the congregation, and they know a whole lot more about their people than anyone else, and the members may know more about the pastor's life than they do each other's lives, but the pastor is always the pastor.

I know I desperately need to be in authentic, mutual community with those with whom I have no complicating professional relationships. Like most pastors, I find it easy to excuse myself from this by saying that I'm too busy with the demands of the church. But busy is boring. Everyone is busy. If my soul is going to remain healthy, I have to have authentic friendships outside of the church. I do have close friendships with other pastors, especially Father

Ted, a Catholic priest in town, and James Kairns, a Pentecostal pastor. I cling to both of these guys.

Ellie and I also made some very close friends with a couple who live a block away from us. They were members of an Episcopal church but got on the wrong side of their priest in a debate about performing the weddings of LGBTQ couples. One night when they were having dinner in our home, they excitedly broke the news that they were planning on leaving their church and joining ours. Ellie cut them off by exclaiming, "The hell you are." And that led me to try to explain all of this. I wasn't very convincing, but they're friends, and so they joined another church because that's what a pastor's friends will do just because they're asked. Or told.

Meanwhile, the planning retreat today gave me a lot of work, and I will enjoy most of it because it will be for the very real people I know, dearly love, and serve as their pastor.

Week Two

Beth, Our New Financial Planner

Ellie and I met with a financial planner today. Her name is Beth. I never wanted to be the kind of person who has a financial planner, and certainly not one I know on a first-name basis. For most of the years there was never enough finances to fret much about planning for more than getting through the next month, while trying to tuck aside what we could for Mackenzie's college education and maybe an inexpensive summer vacation. Eventually we were able to do some modest investing in a mutual fund and we paid off the mortgage early. We didn't need a planner for any of that. Pastors are supposed to have doctors, dentists, and car mechanics like everyone else, but a financial planner? Retirement, however, is a strange new frontier for which we have no expertise. So off we went today in search of some professional help.

Beth the planner was fabulous with all the numbers, pension, Social Security, medical stuff, and charts. So many charts. She of course offered some new financial products, which look interesting. She was pleasant. But she doesn't have a clue how to handle the mystery of pastoral calling at this stage. What I wanted to explain to her is that I'm supposed to be the guy you come to when you're having a hard time understanding what it means to take up your cross and follow Jesus. But there was no explaining. I just kept nodding my head. I realize this is just vain St. Francis wannabe spirituality, but really? A financial planner? Have I already mentioned this confuses me?

It's taken Ellie a while to get me to make this appointment. I'm sure my hesitation has more to do with my resistance to retiring. I know the time is coming, and it's only responsible to have a good plan, but every time she tentatively brings up the topic, I become a whimpering five-year-old boy who goes limp in the grocery store as his mother drags him away from the sugary cereals in those big, beautiful boxes.

Maybe I need a therapist more than a financial planner.

I don't have any messianic illusions about the congregation needing me. I never did. No doubt a fabulous thirty-something-year-old pastor can be found who'll do great in the role I've had the honor of filling for the last twenty-eight years. I'm sure the new pastor will launch into planning retreats with the elders and draft a new mission statement with a series of sermons on it, and at the end of it all print a fabulous new brochure called something like "A City Set on a Hill."

It will all be helpful, mostly by assuring people their church is on the move. I suppose. But the women whose husbands just had a stroke will find themselves on the margins of all that new energy, and the couples whose marriages are unraveling will be riveted by anxieties other than helping the church become more missional, and the kids in the tutoring program that meets in one of our classrooms on Tuesday nights will still mostly just care that their tutors are kind.

It took me a long time to discover that while a church certainly doesn't grow in any sense of that term without a tremendous amount of hard work and imagination from the pastor, the congregation makes it to the Promised Land only by the pastor searching for signs of manna in the fascinating lives of those in and around the church. And then Sunday after Sunday the pastor returns to the pulpit to make holy sense of it all, while those in the pew nod, thinking, "That sounds about right." This quiet, even routine drama eventually becomes more captivating to the pastor than being credited with rebuilding, again, the city set on a hill.

There are no shortcuts for figuring this out. First the pastor has to wander around in the wilderness of planning retreats with lots of visionary devotionals, breakout sessions, and screens filled with fresh new ideas about priorities. Eventually the pastor and congregation discover they've stumbled into the Promised Land. But it wasn't all the careful planning that got us there. It was normal parish life with all its potluck dinners and the 2:00 a.m. frantic phone calls asking me to hurry to the emergency room.

I remember one of my professors in seminary cautioning our class never to confuse the Promised Land with Paradise, which remains lost. The Promised Land isn't a particularly easy place. It's filled with battles, bad ideas, and plenty of opportunities to disappoint our jealous God and each other. But it is the right place for this holy drama to unfold. I've long felt that this congregation was the right place for me, not because it was the best church I could imagine but because it was the one I was given. I know they would say the same about their pastor. We've both been okay with that for a long time, and somehow in spite of our addiction to planning and organizing, God built a holy city on a hill out of our relationships.

I think it was Abraham Heschel who said that when two people come together a holy space emerges between them, and that is where God's creativity occurs. If either of us leaves, so does the holy space. That doesn't mean that I'm critical to the holy work in this congregation. There is always another pastor. But as the meeting with the financial planner made clear today, there is not always another congregation.

Tonight I am wondering where I will go to find my holy space after I am expected to leave the church nursery with the carpet that is stained by God knows what, leave the pastor's office stained by so many confessions and my inadequate counsel, leave the conference room where volunteers exhausted by a long day's work shuffled in so many nights to do the best they could to plan the next thing on our calendar, and leave the pulpit where I kept showing up to say basically the same thing: "Jesus is risen. Who knows what can happen next?"

I've seen so many of my colleagues who have been "honorably retired" from pastoral ministry. I see them flail around trying to figure out the honor of being excused from the congregations where they gave everything that was best about their worn-out lives. There were also those who left angry, cynical, broken, or even disgraced. Those are the stories that make the rounds through clergy meetings. But that doesn't happen as often as our gossip would make it seem. Mostly an old pastor just politely smiles through a retirement celebration in the fellowship hall after worship on the last Sunday. The congregation does the best it can to express a gratitude that is too deep for words. There are a lot of tears. And then the pastor and spouse just wander back out into the wilderness trying to find their next Promised Land.

Over the years some of them have wandered into our congregation as worshipers. The old pastor is always quick to ask me if it's okay, as if she or he might be trespassing. Sometimes we're able to find things for them to do to help us, but usually they are not looking to do much because they're exhausted. Mostly they're just trying to figure out what it means to not be the pastor anymore.

At some point I'm going to have to tell the elders I will be retiring in June. I don't want to be a lame-duck pastor for the rest of the year, but I know I have to give them plenty of notice. Maybe January would be good. That's my least favorite month anyway. No need to screw up Advent.

Beth the planner is very excited about our retirement. At the meeting this morning she praised our various investment and saving schemes over the years, and kept telling us, "You're ready." She doesn't realize this, but essentially she was saying, "June would be a good date for you to head back out into the desert alone with your wife." She thinks that since the money issues have been worked out we'll be fine for the journey.

But that's not the manna we'll need.

Letting Go of Mac the Custodian

Charles McDonald, who goes by Mac, has worked as the church's custodian for almost as long as I've been its pastor. The time had come to nudge him into retirement, which was not my decision. But it was my job to make it happen as carefully as possible.

When I hired him, people weren't sure about the decision because Mac was then a forty-two-year-old ex-convict who had served several years in the state penitentiary for robbing a 7-Eleven. And there were a bunch of serious mistakes, some criminal, before that. One look at his face made it clear that he had known some hard times. His sullen, once-white cheeks had turned permanently ruddy, perhaps from too much alcohol, although that seemed to be behind him by the time he arrived at the church.

Mac had a very progressive parole officer who took an active role in helping him find a job and convinced me to give him another chance. I convinced the personnel committee and disclosed his prison record. But the rules of confidentiality are pretty loose in congregations. The members of the committee confidentially told their spouses, who confidentially told their friends. By the time we announced Mac's new position in the monthly church newsletter, we might as well have placed numbers under his photograph.

There was a bit of murmuring when I hired him, and some questioned the new pastor's wisdom. But our congregation has always prided itself on being socially progressive, and no one wanted to be the hypocrite who said anything resembling "Not in my backyard." I don't feel guilty about leveraging their politics to get him the job.

It took less than a year for everyone in the congregation to become grateful for Mac. He's always been a very private man. He refused to talk about his past, and we knew few details of even his present. What we know is that for over twenty years he always had the snow shoveled off the sidewalks not only on Sunday mornings but also before every evening committee meeting. Anyone needing a supply closet unlocked, or in search of a coffee urn or flip chart, or looking for help setting up some folding chairs and tables knew that Mac was always near. Several asked him how he could walk upright with so many keys dangling from the left side of his belt. He wasn't exactly a happy guy, but he was always pleasant and respectfully referred to people using their last names with Mr. or Miss or Mrs. attached to the front. He never figured out Ms.

But over the years Mac's hard life caught up with him, and it had been difficult for him to keep up with his duties. He had more sick days than our policy allowed, the tile floors were not buffed like they used to be, he moved more slowly when he moved at all, and twice last year the doors weren't open on time for Sunday worship. He lost a lot of the work orders my assistant wrote out for him. His formerly kind nature had soured, and there were several emails about him barking at a parishioner who was just asking for a little help. I don't know what went wrong with him in recent years, but clearly something changed. Maybe it was just too many years.

At the previous personnel committee meeting Mac was the primary topic on the agenda, and they were clear about telling me it was time for Mac to go. This is not the same committee that agreed to hire Mac. It's now filled with younger people who encouraged me to move to an outsourced custodial service that would be more cost effective. Like they have in their offices. Someone only has to say, "We have a fiduciary responsibility to put all the funds we can toward the church's mission," and the pastor's chain has been successfully pulled. And they ever so gently kept telling me that Mac could no longer keep up with the job.

I knew they were right. Beyond the committee's concerns, I had long decided that Mac had somehow lost his ability to love being of service to the congregation, which I expect of all our staff. But I still think about how many times he used to get up at 5:00 in the morning to ensure the sidewalks were clear of snow before the 8:30 early worship service.

Still, I was the one who got Mac his job, and it was my job to get him out of it.

It was easy to convince the personnel committee that they should be generous with his retirement gift, and to let me turn Mac's retirement into a grand celebration. But Mac saw this exit strategy for what it was. We talked about it several times over the last couple of months. At the last meeting he said, "I'm seventy years old. I know I move slower than I used to. But if there are problems, I can do better. This job is my life." I tried to explain about the generous retirement plan the church had arranged. He looked at me like a faithful dog trying to understand as I explained how happy he would be once I set him free in the woods.

The retirement event was an extended coffee hour after worship one Sunday. The chair of the personnel committee and I said some elegant words as Mac stood up in front of the congregation holding his framed certificate of appreciation. Even though he was better at setting up microphones than speaking into them, he said some genuine words of appreciation.

Then he boxed up his few personal effects that remained in the custodian's closet and drove home in his old Ford pickup. I vividly remember waving to him as he drove away out of the church parking lot. That was three months ago.

Today I got a phone call from Mac's daughter, who I didn't know he had, to tell me that he was in the ICU from a stroke and wasn't expected to survive the week. I offered to come immediately to the hospital. She responded, "No, you're the reason he had the stroke. I just need to know if the church had a life insurance policy for him. There're a lot of bills."

If I had to do it all over again, I would probably make the same decision. The church doesn't exist for the staff; we exist for the church. Christians are at their best when they forgive and redeem failures, as our church has a history of demonstrating with its staff, including me. The church did just that with Mac when we hired him so long ago. But if a time comes that any of us can't do our jobs of serving the church, it's time to go.

So why do I keep mulling over this nagging guilt that I really am the reason Mac had a stroke?

Pastoral Lessons from My Sheepdog

I've learned a lot about being a pastor from Esau, our family's hairy sheepdog. The American Kennel Club calls him a bearded collie, but that's misleading since he looks nothing like Lassie. He's actually a Scottish version of the Old English sheepdog, which I believe makes him a Presbyterian.

I have always been uneasy with thinking of myself as the shepherd of our congregation. That role belongs to Jesus Christ. It's far more helpful to think of myself as a sheepdog that nudges sheep toward the only Savior of the flock.

My favorite household chore is to take Esau around the block for his morning walk. We do this as liturgy. As we shuffle along, both of us are waking up to the new day that has come as a grace from God. Esau reminds me to greet the day with excitement.

Without fail at some point in the walk he will stop, stand very still, lift his nose high into the air, and get a sniff of something that excites him so much that his tail is forced to wag. I have no idea what he is sensing, but this morning routine makes me wish I had his nose to receive what I cannot. And I envy his tail that is always eager to express praise for what is out there in creation.

Part of my call as the pastor of a local congregation is to sense the goodness of what is around us, even if a parishioner in a hospital bed cannot. This doesn't mean that I am unaware of the dangers, hurts, and griefs that abound. Neither is Esau. He senses the arrival of a thunderstorm long before anyone in the house, and typically runs for the sanctuary of his crate in the family room. As a pastor, my job is to understand the anxiety that propels our people to gather together at church every Sunday morning in hopes of finding sanctuary from the storms of life. I'm also called to wag with excitement over the discovery that God's grace is always in the air.

Anyone can leave the sanctuary and get a whiff of this, but you have to pay attention. And that's just another reason why we come to worship: to sharpen our spiritual senses.

When Esau and I walk around the block we often encounter another dog. As soon as he sees it approaching, he suddenly lies so flat that he almost disappears into the ground. We didn't train him to do this. Our assumption is that this is instinctive for herding dogs. When they were working the fields caring for the sheep and saw a threat appear, they learned to disappear for a moment to give them time to decide how best to respond.

After our worship services on Sunday mornings, when I am milling around the fellowship hall during coffee hour and see someone coming toward me with resolution in their face, it is critical that I take a few nanoseconds to go flat. This gives me a moment to pray for Spirit-filled guidance on how best to respond to the agenda coming my way. Do I engage? Do I run for the door? Like all sheepdogs I have to be more attentive to the Good Shepherd than to the many other agendas in a congregation. Jesus doesn't call us to take on every need that comes our way.

At the end of December, with the hectic demands of Advent church programs finally over, our family retires for a few days of sabbatical at a winter beach in Delaware. Esau's favorite part of this vacation is the freedom to run unleashed on the empty beach where, like any self-respecting dog, he chases birds. I've noticed over the years that he never runs straight at them. As a herding dog, he runs in an arc to take them by surprise.

Long ago I learned the value of not approaching problem parishioners with head-on confrontation, but by coming at them "slant" as Eugene Peterson calls it. It's ineffective to tell someone, "You have to stop hijacking the worship committee with your personal agendas." More redemption is found by nipping at their heels with the question, "What are you worried about?"

When we take Esau to a dog park, he's the only one who is not having fun; instead, he keeps trying to round up the other dogs. He can't help it. It's just in him to worry about the order of the community. Ministry often isn't fun, and when pastors do find joy it's not because we spent all day chasing Frisbees. Our delight has to come from helping others gather around the Good Shepherd.

Thinking of myself as a sheepdog saves me from the illusion that the pastor is necessary. I am cherished and called by the Shepherd to serve the flock. But I can save no one. Getting off that hook is the best way I know to handle the inevitable failures in ministry and still enjoy a long tenure of service to a congregation.

No pastor survives for long without an intimate devotional life. Even a dog gets this. There are times, usually at the end of the day, when Esau just wants to cuddle up next to his master, get a scratch behind the ears, and hear "Good boy."

October

Week One

Falling from Illusions

Here we are again at World Communion Sunday. One of our previous pastors, Hugh Thompson Kerr, came up with this idea over eighty years ago. Since then there have been lots of good ideas from lots of pastors, but Dr. Kerr had the advantage of being the moderator of the Presbyterian Church when he came up with World Communion Sunday, and so it stuck. At least for our gang.

Dr. Kerr's very good idea was that we should have at least one Sunday a year when we pause to remember that we're in communion with all of the churches around the world. That's important. A few years back I was in Cyprus for the first Sunday in October and mentioned to the Anglican priest at the door following worship that it was an honor to celebrate World Communion Sunday with his parish. He said he'd never heard of it. I tried to explain, and he graciously said every Sunday for them is world communion.

Leave it to the Americans to invent a world-impacting Sunday and forget to ask the world church if this was a good idea.

St. Andrews is so devoted to World Communion Sunday that the church placed a large brass medallion on the floor of the center of the chancel commemorating its emergence from our congregation. Most of the time we use the plate to mark where the choir, pastors, or new members should stand in worship. I doubt that's what Dr. Kerr had in mind.

Last winter Traci Adams, a daughter of the church who grew up in our Sunday school and preschool classrooms, was about to get married. She was so excited to have this wedding in her home church. At the end of the first premarital counseling session she asked if she could show her fiancé Timothy the sanctuary. "Of course," I replied. I led them through a tour of the holy room where countless weddings, funerals, Sunday worship services, and even tedious congregational meetings had taken place.

When we got to the chancel she saw the brass medallion and exclaimed, "Oh Timmy, look at this! This is the place where daylight savings time was invented." Then she turned to me with a look of shock and said, "Wait, that can't be right . . . my *brothers!*" I just smiled gently.

Who knows how many formative memories for kids who grow up in church are actually a weave of biblical stories, church tradition, and stupid stuff your older brothers told you? But learning to navigate the thin line between fact and fiction is part of what it means to be a child of the church.

I grew up hearing that God created the world in seven twenty-four-hour days and that we are all direct descendants of Adam and Eve. My Vacation Bible School teachers may as well have told me that our church invented daylight savings time. It wasn't until I was in college that I learned to look at my past and say, "Wait, that can't be right."

Maybe Dr. Kerr was on to something, and that this is what World Communion Sunday is really all about. It's not our worst idea to have one Sunday every year when we try to join hands with Christians around a family table to say, "There is so much more to God than we thought. We need to keep learning and growing." When we pay attention to the churches around the world, we find Christ in different stories that make us question some of our own church stories. When I listen to Christians from Palestine, India, Africa, or China, I realize how Americanized my theology is. Conversations with these distant relatives always bless me by confusing what was once clear. That really is a blessing.

History has proven that the church is never more wrong than when it is certain it is right. Humility, not certainty, is one of the great virtues.

My calling is not to rush around thrashing the church's misguided ideas. They tend to fall apart if they're not true. It doesn't matter if a pastor discovers that the world doesn't know about our World Communion Sunday, or if a college student discovers evolution and questions the Bible; my calling is to be non-anxious when we're falling from our illusions. It may appear terrifying to discover that a long-cherished conviction is not true, but I've learned that the fall is quite short. Those few inches remind us that we are always bound to God by faith, not by how certain we are of our theology. All the responsible theologians have published articles about how they've changed their mind, and in the end they cherished their faith even more.

Simone Weil once wrote that since Christ is the truth, we should seek the truth even more passionately than we seek him. Because if we seek the truth honestly, we will not travel far before we fall back into his arms.

Over and over again I have stood beside parishioners who were disappointed that God did not answer their fervent prayers. They fell from their illusion that prayer can pull down from heaven any blessing they want. Now they were ready to discover that we can never fall deeper than the Savior who descended even to hell, and who is always waiting to catch us.

The Pastor's Home

Pastors sometimes live in a home that's owned by the congregation they serve. This used to be called a parsonage. Presbyterians call it a manse. No matter what it's called, I like to think of it simply as a place where a parson's family lives. Just before I arrived at St. Andrews the trustees had sold the manses for the pastor and associate pastor and instead provided a housing allowance, in part because the congregation wanted to get out of the real estate business for its pastors, and in part because my predecessors retired from the manse with no equity. Ellie and I have enjoyed owning our own home with no need to check with Alice Matthews or her property committee every time we wanted to make a change in it. But it is still very much a parson's home.

On the wall of the stairwell hang twenty large black-and-white photographs of our ancestors. Half of them are from my wife's family and half from mine. The oldest people on the wall were involved in the Civil War. We hung the photographs in the stairwell because we wanted to be confronted in our coming and going by the reminder that we have a heritage. We call it the Great Cloud of Witnesses Wall.

The stories behind the old pictures are about lost farms; several sons who went away to war and didn't come back; another war with more lost sons; doing whatever it took to survive the Great Depression; a struggle with polio; a young couple who got pregnant too soon; a wife who was beaten by her drunken husband; a couple of pastors who spent their lives anonymously caring for small rural congregations; a daughter who dared to march for suffrage; a wife who left her husband and children to be with her lover and then regretted it; parents who buried their children; and a son who ran away from the farm to join the big bands but then decided he was a farmer after all and returned. It's a mixed story of flawed people who at the end of the day discovered faith was all they had. They faced everything we could possibly encounter, including their own sins. But on Sunday mornings they kept returning to worship to sing about the great faithfulness of their God. That's our family inheritance.

When our daughter Mackenzie was feeling patient, we would tell her the high drama of ordinary faith that was depicted in each family inside the matching frames. These days our grandsons are about as uninterested in all this history as Mackenzie was when she was their age. But when her boys were young and her family still lived nearby, every time she brought them over to our house they would have "wall time" where she would recite the same stories we thought she never learned from us. Recently she's showed us the place in her own home where she's planning on hanging these photos when we totter off to some retirement village.

I also love the wall, and I can't resist a gentle smile as I trudge up the stairs beside it at the end of a long day. I hear their encouragement from the balcony of heaven. When I run down the stairs in a hurry to get to my first appointment of the day, the cloud of witnesses reminds me that there's a bigger story and not to take today's action plan too seriously.

If there were room on the wall, and I had the photographs, I would include the images of Abraham, Moses, David, a prophet or two, maybe the careful Paul, and certainly the impulsive Peter. They're also part of the story of flaws and redemption that runs through our veins as we claim our heritage of being part of the family of Christ.

It is so tempting today to think that since it's a new day, we must self-construct our lives—as if there were no inheritance reminding us who we are, or what our mission in life might be, or how to respond to the hardships of the day. It used to be that home told you who you were, the claims on your life, and the blessings of adversity. Most of the people on the Great Cloud of Witnesses Wall never asked themselves what they would like to do when they grew up. They certainly didn't think of their job as a means of finding fulfillment. All of that was a legacy from their home. But now home is something you're supposed to leave to find yourself.

When Mackenzie graduated from college, the commencement speaker peddled the same drivel I heard when I left school. He didn't mention any notion of a great inheritance of a heritage that makes a claim on our lives. Instead, he looked out over the five thousand graduates and said, "You are the brightest and best we have ever seen. Set your goals high, dream your own dreams, follow your own star, and you can be whoever you want to be." He might as well have said, "Sorry, we have nothing for you. Good luck."

The message to young adults now is that relationships, work, convictions, church, and faith are all just à la carte resources: go down the cafeteria line and choose what you think is best to include on the tray of life. If you don't like your choices, just come back and choose again.

I've spent years of ministry watching my parishioners constantly make another choice about their employment, who they would love, and where they would live—thinking that they would change their lives through these choices. But they were just rearranging the living room furniture. For real change they have to deal with their Creator, who can redeem the hurts of what they received from family and transform them into a mission worthy of their lives. We never get to create our own lives.

I'm not exactly proud of my roots, neither my biological family nor my biblical family that was just as flawed, but I am very thankful that I have them. That's because it's all a story of God's redemption. These roots have kept me from being blown away by the storms of life, because they made it clear to me that there was always more to me than me. The roots also gave rise to a vision of how God's grace works through desperate people who often make mistakes. That theme has found its way into many of my sermons. This heritage has offered me a great faith that I could lean on during the dark nights when my little faith was not enough to get me through. When I could not say that I believe, I could at least believe that we believe.

Why would I sacrifice that incredible heritage for the devil's offer to be whoever I next thought I wanted to be?

The pastor's home should make it clear in our coming and going that we're part of a bigger story that mingles together a daughter's new soccer trophy with a photo of a long-deceased woman who felt called to take to the streets to advocate for giving women the right to vote.

The counsel pastors receive now is to keep work and home separate. It's good advice, of course, but I don't know how far this separation can extend. Even when pastors live in homes they own, the whole congregation knows exactly where the house can be found because most of the members have been in it for dinner parties, new member receptions, the annual Christmas party Ellie and I throw, and staff working retreats. All of that also makes it clear to our family that we're part of a bigger story.

I understand that pastors live with many callings, including the one to family, and the highest one is not to the church but to glorify and enjoy God. But this highest calling has to integrate all the others. How can I with integrity call the church to live out of a greater drama if I'm not working on this at home?

The ministry cannot simply be my profession. I want to be the kind of pastor who really believes Jesus is Lord of all. That has to include my family as much as every other family in the congregation, and every other family whose photograph hangs on our wall. It's easy for me to take off the pastor's collar and just be the husband, dad, or grandfather. But I can never set aside my family's place in the great biblical drama of redemption. While I'm never the pastor to my family, it was always one of my callings to work beside my wife to create a home that inculcates what we believe.

I probably do that best when I make mistakes that my family has learned to forgive. Just like they forgive each other. Again.

That's just how our family story goes.

The Grace of Being Ordinary

Alexander Edison emailed a few days ago to ask if I would be a reference for his application to Harvard. I asked him to come and talk to me about this.

His hands were trembling a bit as he told me about how important this was to his parents. I asked if this was important to him (such a pastor thing to do). His shoulders and head went down. Then he said, "I just have to get into this college. Can you write a letter to tell them something about my involvement in last year's mission trip to Guatemala?"

Alexander is an eighteen-year-old member of the congregation who was raised by his attorney parents to make it into Harvard so he would become even more impressive than they were professionally. I baptized him when he was a baby. I saw him in our Sunday school classes with that same shoulder and head fallen countenance when he didn't know the answer to the teacher's question about Noah's ark. I looked out my window in the church office to see him tentatively waiting for one of the cool kids to choose him in kickball. I've known Alexander his whole life and have watched him grow up in our congregation into a fabulous young man who always seems to have doubts about himself.

It's hard to know how to help a high school senior who realizes he's never going to be the idol his parents have tried to shape. He's a wonderfully average teenager who is filled with typical concerns—like finding the courage to ask a girl to prom, which was the next topic he brought up after we got done with Harvard.

He's more gifted than he realizes, and I certainly don't know his future, but he doesn't show the early signs of being a genius who will someday receive a Nobel Prize. And he knows it. His parents take their ambitions for him as a sign of love, but Alexander really just wants to be eighteen. And hopefully make his parents at least satisfied with him. I don't know if that's possible. They're breaking down his young soul with the expectation to be extraordinary.

We don't get to be young and ordinary for very long, and we certainly don't appreciate the fleeting moment while we have it. Mostly, that's because kids get bombarded with questions about what they are going to do with their lives, but teenagers realize what's really being asked of them: "How will you achieve being spectacular?" Even high schools elevate those who are stars in athletics, academics, and popularity. But that scale is so local and so limited that it boils down to who is the best of the very ordinary kids the world has never heard of. And yet that's the gift.

For a little while longer this eighteen-year-old boy should get to hide behind his youth. At this point his achievements are mostly just about his potential, and his sins are pretty boring. All of the interesting decisions are still before him, and he's nowhere near the second half of life where he will have to deal with the consequences of those decisions. He doesn't yet wake up every morning regretting what he's done and left undone. People are not yet depending on him for their own lives to work well. If he's going to make a difference in the world, it will come through thousands of small, faithful, ordinary choices he makes along the way in life, not because an Ivy League school chose him.

I have no idea if he'll get into Harvard, or if he should, but I do know that someone needs to convince him that it really doesn't matter. I gave it my best shot to explain this, but Alexander couldn't hear it. He left my office as burdened as when he arrived, saying, "I've got to get into this school." It's still striking to me that he's never said, "I want to get into this school."

I live with regret about my own ambitions and how much they cost me and the people I love. But after the conversation with Alexander it occurred to me that it's a whole different burden to live up to the ambitions that your parents place on you to be extraordinary. I would rather struggle with whatever is going on inside that drives me.

My parents had zero ambitions for me. There was never a conversation about what college I might attend or who in the world would pay for it. There were too many arguments between them, followed by too much silent treatment, and way too much preoccupation with their own lives that weren't working out as they had hoped. It never occurred to them to ask themselves if they were prepared to send either of their sons to even a community college.

Which is the easier cross to bear? Being Alexander with parents breathing down his neck, or being the kid who's figured out he's on his own to do the best he can? I'll take my own cross. But the ambition thing will ultimately work against him as much as it did me. And then there is the grace of finally embracing ordinary. It's just a shame that it takes so many years to get there.

The Study

It was another long day.

Alice Matthews came into the church office to see me without an appointment to complain about the new custodian I hired last month. I was pretty sure we had retired Alice from the property committee.

Gladys Riley and her daughter came to ask me to join them for an intervention that would demand her husband Gene give up his driver's license after the last fender bender. "I just know he's really going to hurt someone if we don't do something," she whispered.

Immediately afterward there was a long appointment with one of our worshipers I didn't know well who only wanted to complain that our church doesn't have an American flag, which had actually never occurred to me. While he yammered on, I was still thinking about old Gene Riley, and how hard it was going to be to take away his driver's license.

There was a long trip to the hospital to visit Brad Davis, who chaired my search committee so many years ago, and who stood beside me during an early building campaign fiasco, and who always said yes to anything I asked no matter how many times I called. He had been struggling with a heart murmur. I fought my way across town and over two congested bridges to get to the hospital, only to discover that he had just been discharged. I was too late. That will be "no problem" to Brad, but deeply disappointing to his wife.

And there were so many emails that kept proliferating at the speed of light, as if that was the only miracle I would see that day, and they were all expecting an empathetic reply within hours.

Oh yeah, and our director of youth ministries stuck his head in my door to say that he had been contacted by a larger church and just wanted to give me a heads-up that he might be interviewing for a new position.

Then I finally got home. There was a fabulous dinner prepared by my wife, who had found yet another new kale recipe. She offered more than one "Are you okay?" at the table. I kept changing the subject asking about her day, the plumber's success with the toilet, what I heard on NPR driving home, finding relief in anything that didn't involve the church. This is how I exhale and return to some sense of normality. It made me happy to hear how happy she is with a new client, and even happier to hear about her phone conversation with Mackenzie, who now lives on the West Coast.

After dinner I washed the dishes, assuring her I was fine. "No worries." When I was done with the last dirty pot, and the conversation about the water heater was over, she gave me a hug and said with a smile, "Okay, you can go now." And off I went to The Study.

I fully realize how costly that is to her. She would much prefer that we spend the night watching an old movie cuddled up together on the sofa. But that has seldom worked out well. The movie is usually an important film, and I usually fall asleep, sometimes even snoring, and that leads to a long and familiar conversation the next day. I'm really bad at movies. Alone in The Study I'm fully awake again.

It would be saying too much to assume she's forgiven me for this, but she's clearly surrendered to it. And the grace behind, "Okay, you can go now," is never lost on me. The irony is that she worked hard to design and decorate the room where I go to be alone and to write the sermons, lectures, articles, and an occasional book as I try to figure out what God is doing in the lives of the people at St. Andrews.

The walls of The Study are filled from floor to high ceiling with the thousands of religious books I've collected over the years. Their insights have changed the world. They surround me like a community of old scholars who urge me on through every challenging new sermon, lecture, article, or book I'm writing. The huge desk came from somewhere in Italy, and I can't tell you why that's important to me, but our wedding picture parked on the corner reminds me of the day my wife said, "I'll love you no matter what." Her vow might as well have said, "I love you even though you need your lonely place to mend your soul again every night."

The shade on the desk lamp hangs a bit crooked, but I won't let her fix it. The Study even has a fireplace that doesn't work, which I resist turning into a metaphor. The large rug bears the marks of three of our successive dogs that have slept away on it while I was frantic at the Italian desk trying to find a better adverb. And the smell . . . the smell is of Captain Black Pipe Tobacco, my favorite vice.

The Study is the antioffice. There are no committee meetings in it, and nobody comes there to complain or even to have a strategy meeting about those who are complaining.

Few people in the church have seen The Study, and—this is important—few want to. It would seem too voyeuristic to the grown-ups in the church. They want me to have a place where I go to bathe in whatever insights I can find so that I'll have something to say on Sunday, but they certainly don't want to watch me do it. They just assume that like all healthy adults I know what I have to do to take care of myself.

Though my wife understands the importance of The Study, thankfully she doesn't honor it very much. She often walks through the closed door and sits at the chair she bought me as a Christmas gift years ago and talks about whatever is on her mind. Those are always the best moments of my day.

I need The Study. But I can't stay there. The purpose of a sanctuary is to find the holy wind that'll sail you back to the people you love.

Week Five

"It Hurt My Feelings"

A twentysomething member of the church came to see me today at the church office. When he made the appointment, he said he had something "really important" to discuss. The moment he shuffled through the door I could tell we weren't going to have much small talk.

He plopped down in the chair across from me, looked down as he began wringing his hands, and got to the point. "Several of my friends recommended me to be an elder in the church, but the nominating committee didn't even put my name before the congregation."

Without thinking about the possible subtext of this, I responded too quickly: "Well, the committee receives a lot more recommendations for new elders than they can include on the slate of nominations. They make their choices by discerning who can meet specific needs before the congregation these days. Their decision not to nominate you certainly wasn't personal."

Immediately his countenance changed from troubled to angry. "Well it sure feels personal," he shot back. Then after a pregnant pause he teared up and said, "And it hurt my feelings." After that he got up and stormed out of my office.

In the end, his complaint was that the church hurt his feelings. Not that we were unjust, or the system was rigged, or even that we were discriminating against young white males. Nope. The concern was that the standard bureaucratic process of finding the next slate of officers wasn't careful with his feelings.

After this abrupt appointment, I remained in my chair stunned by his lament. The church hurt his feelings? So what? The church hurts my feelings almost every day. At its best we're a community of flawed sinners whose aspirations are higher than not hurting each other, but along the way we inevitably do exactly that.

Where did he get the impression that our congregation was supposed to affirm him? Did his ever-attentive parents make him feel a bit too special? Has he never read a newspaper or actually seen the beggar asking for a bit of change? Has he heard nothing about the gospel I have been preaching all these years? Or was it drowned out by this newer gospel that has made personal affirmation something of an inalienable right?

Of this I am sure: The mission of the church is not to create an alternative society where you never have to experience rejection, loss, or hurt. Our mission is to draw people to the grace of God. As often as possible we try to do that by affirming people's gifts and the beauty of their faithfulness to life's callings. But those celebrations are few, and they have a very short shelf life on the soul. Frankly, the flawed church's proclivity to disappoint each other is better at drawing people to the grace of God.

The deep affirmation this young man is yearning to find can only come by seeing the heavens open to proclaim, "You are my beloved with whom I am so pleased." This is his real identity in Christ. The church can echo that at times, but we cannot give him a better reason to have good feelings than the one heaven has offered. Nor should we.

85

November

The Sin I Can't Forgive

I received a letter from Mackenzie today. Few people still write letters, so it pleases me enormously that she puts pen to paper when it would be so much easier for her to email or text. She knows I'm buffeted by electronic messages.

Her letter didn't say anything extraordinary. It was mostly about her delight in the latest activities of her kids, who are the center of her life. What's extraordinary is that she wants to write to me at all. I wasn't a great father.

Our home life was always warm and loving. And Mackenzie always seemed to enjoy growing up in the pastor's home, entering into all the church events we hosted. But there were so many of her soccer games and ballet recitals and orchestra concerts I missed when I was at some church committee or board meeting that seemed so important at the time. Mackenzie was always forgiving. But I take her grace as a judgment. When she was still young and formative, I taught her to be quick to forgive my failures before there could be any angry adolescent rage about me not showing up for her very often.

I would love to say my absence as her father came out of my calling to be a faithful servant of the church, but I now doubt that

Jesus was impressed by my focus on working so hard for him. From the moment I cradled her in my arms after her birth I was crazily devoted to her, but I missed the devotion to spending deliciously ordinary time with her.

I've tried to take some comfort in knowing that her mother was there for her when I was not, but that only adds more judgment that clings to my soul.

I've also tried telling myself I was just trying to be a good provider. That drive has been with me a long time. As I was turning seventeen I discovered I was homeless. That's not because I left home but because my parents' marriage fell apart, and they took off in different directions on their own. My older brother interrupted his college studies to get a construction job and help support me. I worked at the local Hess gas station. We knew that if we didn't work we were going to be hungry on the streets, which should not be in the forefront of a teenager's anxieties. I remember swearing to myself that I would never let my child be in such a terrifying place. Lots of therapy has helped me confront this motivation behind my workaholic tendencies, but I still have to live with my accusation that I hurt my daughter. No child wants a father who is too busy being a reliable provider that he doesn't have time to be a reliable dad.

To make matters worse, I wasted the fleeting years I had with her at home by badgering her into becoming someone who was careful, professional, maybe even a leader of the church, when she really wanted to be an artist. Trying to get it really right as a father, I got it really wrong.

Mackenzie long ago stopped thinking of herself as my ignored blessing. I don't know how she did it, but she's clearly recovered from all the wounds I inflicted along her way.

I know enough about the gospel to realize that nothing redemptive comes from settling into judgment. But I cling to this particular judgment and cannot let it go no matter how much absolution my child tries to give me. I refuse to be forgiven for this sin. And this ever-looming judgment is one of the ways I understand the burden of guilt my parishioners insist on carrying.

Finding Gravitas
When You're Young

We have a young seminary intern working with our congregation named Pendleton. Not Penn. He's actually Pendleton III, but
blessedly he leaves out "the third" part. He's privileged but not
arrogant. His grandfather started a furniture manufacturing business that his father now runs. His mother is a college librarian.
He's clearly smart and strikingly handsome, but he doesn't seem
to be aware of these gifts. I often see him running like a gazelle,
when I am walking, in the park. He seems to have it all.

Early in his internship I asked him to tell his story at a parish
staff meeting. Mostly it was just a tribute to his family, his home
church, and his clarity about wanting to be a pastor since he was
in junior high school. I kept waiting for the "I once was lost" part
of the typical Amazing Grace testimony, but it never came. Now
I realize he wasn't hiding it. Pendleton has no idea what it means
to be lost.

All pastors have to sacrifice something to accept their call to
the ministry. Most of us have to give up our other plans for life,
our failures, self-doubts, fears, cherished wounds, or regrets over

our prodigal debacles in life. Pendleton has to give up being the third generation of elder brothers who have always made the right choices. If he can't get over that, he's going to be way too irritating for our line of work.

The question is, how does the church help this young man find the gravitas he's going to need to be a pastor? It can come, in part, from the great theological tradition of faith he has inherited. I know he will study it well, but I hope he can embrace the last two thousand years of the church's dreams, failures, and redemption as his own story. And he can find some weightiness to his soul by looking at his own life more critically. Like all elder brothers, his besetting sin is not riotous living but trusting in his carefully constructed life. Sin is anything that separates us from God, and nothing will do that with more damage to the soul than trying to be your own savior. But mostly, his soul will find gravitas by embracing the hurts of his parishioners.

This afternoon Pendleton reported to me on his visit to Mrs. O'Donohue, who has been in the hospital after her last surgery for what is probably terminal lung cancer. It was his first solo pastoral call. I had taken him with me a few times when I was making hospital visits, as had our associate pastor. He had even gone with me to see Mrs. O'Donohue earlier in the week. But this time there was no one between him and the person in the bed except Jesus.

Pendleton is without guile, so he had no trouble giving me a self-critical depiction of what happened on this visit. He began by saying he went to the hospital reassuring himself that he knew how to do this, but he prayed that he wouldn't say anything stupid. "That was your prayer?" I interrupted. "That you wouldn't say anything stupid?" He held up a hand and said, "I know. Can you believe it? I wasn't even thinking about Mrs. O'Donohue." I sat back in my chair, resolved to stop interrupting.

"When I got to her room at the hospital, the door was shut so I waited outside. And the wait was pretty long. But I didn't want to just knock on the door and barge in." Again I interrupted, "Why not?" His face grimaced when he said, "Who knows what was going on in there?" After a pause, he continued, "Anyway, a nurse came by and asked if she could help me. I told her that I was from the church and I was here to see Mrs. O'Donohue. Then she said, 'Well, honey, she's not out here in the hall.'"

"The nurse opened the door for me to go into the room. Mrs. O'Donohue was lying in bed watching TV. I stood back because I didn't want to get in the nurse's way, but I said hello, reintroduced myself to her, and tried to ask her about the show she was watching. She was barely looking at me when she responded. Then the nurse finished whatever she was doing with that monitor-thing, and said to Mrs. O'Donohue, 'Why don't I turn off the TV so you can talk to your pastor?' Then I said that I was just in seminary and an intern at the church. And that I was only there because you sent me. Honest, I wasn't pretending."

"Clearly," I interrupted yet again.

"When the nurse left, I asked Mrs. O'Donohue how she was feeling and like immediately she started crying. I didn't know what to do. I asked if she wanted me to get the nurse to come back. But she shook her head no. Then I just sat there like a dope. But when I asked her if I could pray for her, she really surprised me when all she said was, 'My daughter hasn't been to see me. I wasn't a very good mother. Can you pray for her?' She said nothing about the cancer, surgery, hospital, or how sick she is. She was just really upset about her daughter. This happened two days ago, but I've got to tell you I can't stop thinking about it."

Pendleton and I began to unpack some of the critical insights he was discovering. The nurse taught him to be a professional in the hospital, where he belongs as much as she does. Young pastors often envy the doctors and nurses who have uniforms, stethoscopes around their necks, pills to pass out, and monitors to, well, monitor. Everything about them announces that they have serious work to do. So does the pastor. It was Pendleton's very serious job to listen to Mrs. O'Donohue and to place her broken heart into the hands of God. Even the nurse knew that. In time, he'll believe it too.

He also learned never to make assumptions about the response he'll get when he asks a person in tears, "Can I pray for you?" There is a lot of subtext to tears, and it may have nothing to do with the reason someone is in the hospital. But just the offer to pray is an invitation for the parishioner to ask their pastor to grapple with their real issues before God.

The most important legacy of Pendleton's visit with Mrs. O'Donohue was the discovery that if he is called to be a pastor, then he's stuck with her. He will return to his studies at the seminary, but during the lectures he'll keep thinking about that old woman who is brokenhearted because, of all her bad choices in life, the one that brings her to tears is whatever she did to make her daughter too angry to see her while she is wasting away in a hospital. He'll think about it again when he sees a young mother holding the hand of a young child who still trusts her. He'll think about it in his daily prayer time when he starts to reveal his own soul before God and finds Mrs. O'Donohue waiting there as well.

All of that will leave him "lost" in her heartache. Then he'll start to look around for the Amazing Grace.

Week Three

The Pastor on the Doctor's Table

Dr. Sawyer is a cantankerous old physician and the last professional in my life who's my age. I find his grumpiness strangely comforting. He typically looks at the lab results after my annual physical, and says, "You're fine. Put your clothes on and get out of here. I've gotta take care of some sick people." Sometimes he even tells me to stop bothering him. I just love that.

Ellie was a bit worried about a mole on my arm that seemed to be growing. After the eighth time she asked me about it, I made an appointment to see Dr. Sawyer—or old Doc Sawbones, as Ellie calls him. I fully expected him to roll his eyes at me and say, "You again?" But he took one look at the odd growth and immediately started typing something on a laptop. "I'm worried about this thing. I just sent an email to the best dermatologist in the city. My assistant will give you her number. You should call her as soon as possible." That couldn't be good.

The dermatologist, who has a faculty appointment at the medical school in town, and who's younger than my daughter, focused on the funny spot too long and said, "We're going to need to run some tests." Actually it was me who ran through the tests.

What followed was a lot of waiting rooms, and getting poked with really big needles, and riding under MRI machines that made strange "tsk tsk" clicking noises at me, as if I did something wrong to be lying there beneath its pending judgment.

After all that, a doctor I had never met before came into the stark room where I had been sitting alone too long to say, "You have metastatic melanoma." He dialed up the results of the tests on a computer screen and pointed to a bunch of dark blotches that were on my lungs. "Even though it's spreading, you have a good chance of surviving this with treatment. But there are no guarantees." Then he said, "I'm sorry," and walked out.

There I sat on an examination table lined with butcher paper, trying to absorb every word that came at me too fast. I would love to say I immediately began to pray. But actually I just sat there wondering how I would explain this to Ellie. I thought, first, of the best way to reveal to her my diagnosis, and second, about how to console her when she became upset. And I knew she would hate the second part almost as much as the first. But I couldn't protect her or Mackenzie from this.

Then I started thinking about the congregation, and that made me literally nauseous—out of concern that some of them would put it on Facebook, and then I'd be publicly reduced to a prayer request. This is not how I want to end my long ministry at the church.

It's been three days now since I had the "I'm sorry" conversation with the doctor I don't know. I hardly have my head around it, and at my insistence my wife and I haven't told anyone yet. Maybe we will, but I need to protect this horrible news for now. I've never been able to explain this tendency in me, but I just need to hold on to something that's awful and threatening before I give it away to the compassion of others.

Tonight, amid the big questions banging around in my head, I wonder why at the end of hard conversations with doctors my hope is always placed in the hands of their assistants who pass me off to someone else so I'm no longer their problem. "After all," the busy doctors think, "my assistant gave him a phone number to call." I can't imagine telling one of my parishioners, "I'm sorry your wife left you, and that you're wondering where the hell is Jesus. My assistant will give you the phone number of someone who may be able to help." And then I could just walk out the door with a brief apology, leaving them on butcher paper.

Ellie can't stop crying. I keep explaining that with treatment I may be able to beat this. But she's already gone through all of the five stages of grief in three nights, and I'm pretty sure it's not supposed to work that fast. The "blaming" was the most interesting part of her journey. After spending two hours online last night she discovered we weren't using the right sunscreen on the church's last mission trip to Guatemala. "The customer reviews of this sunscreen are terrible. And a class action lawsuit is pending." But she and everyone else on the work team were working beside me, and I'm the only one to show up with melanoma, so I don't think we can blame the sunscreen we passed around, or Guatemala, or any other scapegoat.

The search for a scapegoat has been around for a long time. If my memory is right, somewhere in Leviticus—not a book of the Bible where I spend a lot of time—there's an instruction to lay the sins of the people on a goat that is then sent out into the desert wilderness away from the community. And then somehow the goat is found and sacrificed. Rough day for the goat. But clearly the story illustrates that we have long looked for something or someone to blame for our problems. Or explain them. Or make sure they're gone, sacrificed, and can't come back.

I don't blame anyone, anything, myself, or even God. It's only been three days. I haven't even become upset or afraid. I am mostly focused on letting it sink in that I have a lethal disease. At this early stage I sit in The Study looking around at the two thousand years of Christian wisdom on my bookshelves and wonder what the scholars have to say that's more substantial than "I'm sorry."

I've read these books carefully, and I've even taken doctoral exams on some of them. But tonight it occurs to me that they weren't writing their theologies to explain why an old pastor would get cancer. They spent their lives thinking about greater questions, like how is God cleaning up the mess we've made of everything? And actually that's how I've spent my life as well, only mostly with one person at a time.

At this point I'm thinking, I just got cancer, which is the most absurd disease nature could have dreamed up because it's my own terrorist cells that are on the hunt for my life. I'm never going to figure out something so irrational. And God? Well, the Holy has never been big on explanations.

Several years ago I officiated at a funeral for a man who crashed his small Cessna plane. At the reception I wandered into several conversations with his friends who were mostly trying to figure out what he may have done wrong—as if they would be secured from ever having such a horrible end to their lives if they were more careful. I keep pondering that tonight. I remember how odd it was that this was the best response they could muster in response to the death of a friend. In my mind I keep interrupting their so-missing-the-point conversation by asking, "How about cancer? What's your careful plan to avoid a stupid mole on your arm that could kill you?"

But my conversations with Ellie are not at all imagined. They are tear-streaked and omnipresent, even when she takes a break to go back to the Mustang and I to The Study. This disease interrupted my life, and she may never be the same as a result. We had carefully saved and suffered through all those irritating meetings with the financial planner, and spent so many nights on the deck behind the house wolfing down popcorn while debating our dreams for retirement—and now for the first time we are both having to think about what it will be like if the time comes for her to plan a future without me.

I can't imagine not being there if she is. And that's all I need to make the phone call to the oncologist so I can begin the treatments. I'll figure out the meaning of this along the way.

Week Four

The Pastor's Pastor

Father Ted and I met at Starbucks this afternoon, as we have twice a month for the ten years since he attended a doctor of ministry seminar I taught at the seminary.

He's a Roman Catholic priest. We've jointly officiated at several wedding services together, and when the service is held in his church, he stands before us in his splendid white alb adorned with a stunning stole and says, "Now we've come to the point of the wedding for receiving the Sacrament. We all know that one of the people before us is Catholic and the other is Protestant. Today the sanctuary is filled with both types of Christians. You're all welcome to come forward to receive the body and blood of Christ because, just like this couple kneeling before us, we all need all the grace we can receive." And there I would deferentially stand about two steps behind him at the altar in my black-sheep Protestant robe, eager to be the first to taste the means of grace he was about to place on our tongues. I'm pretty sure Rome frowns on such hospitality at the altar. And that makes his offer of grace all the more precious.

Father Ted is fifteen years younger than I am. There's a part of me that thinks it's ridiculous to call someone "Father" who was my student and is named Ted. But it works for both of us. He's clear about his identity as a priest, and I'm clear about my need to hitchhike on the Catholic tradition at times in order to find a confessor.

Most of our discussions over lattes are not all that vulnerable. We share our professional anxieties, although while he allows me to think of our relationship as a friendship, it's clear to both of us that he's always wearing a collar while I'm not. At least not around him. I love that. Whenever I need him to drop the friendship facade and listen to my confession, he leans forward and knows all the right responses.

I feel bad that I take more than I give in this relationship. But Father Ted seems to have come to terms with that long before he met me. I have no idea who he goes to for his priest. When I've asked about that, he just smiles and says, "We've got it covered." I hope that's true.

Today I broke the news to him that I had this metastasized cancer. He was visibly jarred by the news, and it looked like his eyes were tearing up as he probed for more medical information. Like a friend, he asked about how Ellie was handling this, how I thought it would affect my work, and what he could do. Then his countenance changed as he went into priest mode, paused, and asked, "So, how have your conversations with God been going about this?" And that's what I most needed from Father Ted because there have been no conversations between God and me about this disease.

My tradition in the Christian faith strongly affirms the doctrine of the priesthood of all believers. A respectable Protestant theologian would read this diary entry and say that any believer could have and should have asked the same question. I absolutely agree. But I needed a real priest in a collar today. That's something Protestants may understand emotionally but never theologically. Including me. Still, I drove home so relieved that I had talked with my priest who cautioned me to be careful about giving God the silent treatment.

I've taken on Father Ted's priestly role with my parishioners, even though neither they nor I nor my tradition could explain the dynamics. But when the road you're traveling is terrifying, and the relentless wind is scattering tree limbs carelessly, you need more than family, a friend, or theology. You even need more than your own prayer life that's a flickering flashlight that has stopped working. On the dark nights you need a priest.

I don't need to be thought of by my own parishioners as a priest in order to take comfort in realizing that, within all those sermons, committee meetings, counseling sessions, and mission trips, I really have been a type of priest to my parishioners. I refuse to be called "Father," and my parishioners would never stop giggling if the next revision to the Presbyterian Book of Order suggested it. But I've spent my life being the oddly other person, not quite a friend, who maintains someone else's holy conversation.

Today I got a glimpse of just how important that is to the soul. Even if Father Ted had not asked the exact right question, but instead said something benign or silly, I still would have found enormous comfort just in telling my priest that I'm starting treatment for a pretty scary disease.

Not to sound like too much of a Protestant work ethic cliché, but the hardest part of what lies ahead is not the painful medical treatments. And it's certainly not the actual loss of my life. The hard part is going to be the hard work of caring for all the people I love who'll be trying to care for me. But I'm not going to travel this road well without my priest who keeps nudging me back to my God.

Like Father Ted said, I have to start talking to the Holy about this not just for the sake of my own soul. Others are counting on me. Five minutes into the sermon, everyone in the congregation can tell if God and I are still on speaking terms.

I get it that Jesus is my true great high priest. And he's the true priest to everyone I've served over all these long years of ministry. But sometimes you need a person in front of you in a latte-stained, rumpled shirt to be your flawed glimpse of Jesus carrying you back to God. As I think about my retirement, I hope I've spent my life being Father Ted by offering anyone "all the grace we can receive."

Humility to the End

Joe Lincoln was a forty-nine-year-old member of the congregation's cancer support group, the Barnabas Circle. We set up the
group three years ago when we realized we had an unusually high
number of parishioners at some stage in cancer treatment. Several
of them had asked me if the church could pull together a place
where it was easier to talk about the spiritual aspects of their difficult journey than it was with their families and friends.

The group meets with me every other week. We usually have
twelve to fifteen people attending. There's really not much of a
program. I start off the meetings with a brief devotional from a
biblical text, and then we just go around the circle. People can say
whatever is on their minds, but no one is allowed to respond with
advice. The goal is to be companions, like Barnabas was with Paul
when he was getting stones thrown at him. Joe Lincoln helped
organize the circle and only missed a meeting if it conflicted with
his treatments for leukemia.

He had good seasons with the disease and hard ones, up and
down, for the last three years. He was in a clinical trial for a while that
offered a sliver of hope. But the news just kept getting worse. A couple of months ago the doctors recommended suspending treatments

because the disease was progressing too rapidly to continue. He said goodbye to the specialists, and his wife called hospice.

When Joe showed up at the Barnabas Circle after that decision was made, he used his turn to speak to describe what it means to learn that you're going to die soon. It was striking to hear him say that he never much cared for the "battle" language others used when they talked about their fight with cancer. And he certainly didn't want to think that he was now losing the battle for his life. The way he saw it, his life was just coming to an end, like all lives do. He was eager to do all that science could offer to sustain his life, and he was willing to put up with all the chemo and feeling lousy in order to be responsible with his life. But he said he was never fighting for it. "In order to have a battle, there has to be an enemy," he said, "but who or what is the enemy here? It's cancer. My own cells that are shutting down my life. So this is just me— coming to an end. It's sooner than I want, but for God's sake, literally, we should have enough humility to know we don't get to determine when we die."

It was good that we had a rule no one was allowed to give advice when a speaker was done, because there was nothing to say after Joe was done. But those words about humility were going to stick with us for a long time. Joe had been a partner in a large law firm in town. We all knew he had a reputation for being hard hitting, even at church. For him to prefer the language of humility over battle was huge. Clearly, he had been doing a lot of work on his soul lately.

Six weeks ago it looked like Joe's life was over. He had attended to legal matters to ensure his wife would be financially okay. He handwrote long letters to people all over the country who were important to him. And he made an appointment with me to talk about his funeral. He was ready. Then one night it looked like his organs were failing. His wife told me to come to the hospital as soon as possible.

As I got there a couple other members of the Barnabas Circle were leaving his room. He smiled when I walked in, held up his hand to take mine, and with a raspy voice said, "Looks like this is it." Through her tears, his wife said their kids were on the way from the colleges they attended, and she hoped they would arrive in time. We had an extraordinary last conversation between a pastor and parishioner. Humility had become his favorite topic, and he used the theme again to tell me that everything he cherished in life came not as his achievement but as God's blessing. He looked over at his wife and said, "Especially her." Then he looked hard at me and said, "Isn't it great that we don't control our lives? I now realize I could never have achieved anything as good as I've received." I prayed my thanksgiving for his extraordinary life and reminded God that Jesus said he had prepared a place for this humble disciple. After embracing his wife and telling her to call me any time, I left thinking I had rarely seen someone die so well.

Only Joe didn't die.

I called his hospital room the next day expecting to speak with his wife or a nurse, but to my surprise it was Joe who picked up the phone. He said it was strange but he seemed to be rallying, and he was actually feeling pretty good. I told him I would stop by later that day. By the time I got there several of the machines that had been in the room the night before were gone, and Joe was sitting up in bed. "Still here," was all he said with a shrug. I smiled and said, "Well, that's great news. At least it gives your kids time to get here." Joe smiled and said he was thankful for that. The kids arrived and had some important conversations with their dad. On the fourth day, the attending physician at the hospital said Joe could go home. And the kids went back to school.

Three weeks later the same thing happened again. There was another round of goodbyes. More tears and hugs in the hall outside his hospital room, with all of us remarking how bravely he was facing the end. Another trip home from college. And again, a few days later Joe went home.

When his wife called last week, she was almost apologetic when she told me that Joe had collapsed at home and the ambulance was taking him to the hospital. When I got there I found that this time he was in the ICU. He pulled the oxygen mask off his mouth just to say, "This is starting to get embarrassing." He began coughing as he laughed.

I just got home from conducting his funeral. One of his friends in the Barnabas Circle gave the eulogy. He quoted from Joe's homily to the group—the part about that for God's sake, literally, we should have enough humility to know we can't determine when we will die. Then he said, "Joe was so big on humility that he was ready when he was so certain he was going to die. But just to mess with his certainty, God made him live six weeks longer. Apparently life is a humility to the end."

I haven't told anyone in the church yet about my own cancer. The logical place to start would be the Barnabas Circle. But I was supposed to be the only one in the group who was healthy. I wasn't there as a participant in their disease; I was just being the pastor.

"Apparently life is a humility to the end." Joe is probably leaning over the balcony of heaven to tell his pastor that's good news. I'm working on it.

December

Our Faith and My Faith

Jeff Castleberry came to see me today, at my invitation. Last Tuesday night he raised a question about the Apostles' Creed in our new members class, and it was clear that he wasn't buying my response. So I asked him to stop by the office where we could discuss his concerns more fully.

Jeff is in his early sixties, I would guess. It took us a while to get to his pressing theological question because I asked him first to tell me a bit more about himself. He began not by telling me what he did for a living—the typical response to that question—but by saying he was once very involved in a church in a different state. He went through a rough divorce and subsequently moved to our town several years ago. Getting involved in another church was not high on his priority list because he had been disappointed in how his previous church community had responded to both him and his ex-wife when their marriage was unraveling. "I just needed a break from church," was how he put it.

"But now you are in our new members class," I responded. "Why is that?"

He looked at the floor a while before saying, "I dunno. I guess I just miss worship. I've been feeling unmoored for the last few years since I moved here, and so I started worshiping at St. Andrews a couple of months ago. I came to your class just to learn a bit more about the church, but I'm not sure I'm the kind of guy you want to have as a member."

"Why is that?"

"Well, that's why I was asking about the Apostles' Creed you all say every Sunday. In my last church we didn't have to do that. And while I really love your worship services, I don't like being told what I have to recite as my beliefs. I'm an engineer and not a theologian, so I have to admit that I don't understand all of the creed, but I do have my doubts about some of it. Like the virgin birth stuff. And Jesus descended into hell? What's that about?"

I've had this conversation enough times to know better than to launch into exegesis about the creed. So instead I asked him to tell me more about why he decided to start coming to a worship service again.

"You mean the unmoored thing?" Jeff asked.

"Yes, help me understand that."

"Well, I moved to this town to take a new job, thinking it might be good to get a fresh start in a place where I'm not known. But I'm not married anymore, and I'm not exactly the kind of guy women want to date. My kids and I talk on the phone sometimes, but they're pretty busy with their own lives. It isn't that I'm lonely, really. I don't mind living alone. But I feel like I'm just showing up every day at a life that isn't really about anything. Or anyone else. I like my job, but it's not like I'm doing anything that really makes a difference. So I thought I would try recovering some sense of spirituality by coming back to church. But this creed thing really bugs me."

The window into his soul didn't stay open long, but it was just enough for me to offer some suggestions about the subtext of our conversation.

Jeff is a victim of the popular illusion that it's up to you to as-semble your life, and the best way to do that is through making choices. Including the choice about what you believe. If the life you've self-constructed in one place falls apart, you just have to make more choices that will allow you to rebuild a life. And if this new life is still vaguely dissatisfying, it may help to look for a little spirituality. But on your own terms, like all your other choices. The deep problem with this strategy is that we're not the creator of our lives. We inherit life from the tradition of the Great Faith we've received.

My challenge was to help Jeff see that the thing that "bugs" him the most about our worship services is probably what he most needs in his life—an old creed that he didn't write but still professes as his own. It is how we stay moored in life.

What the soul needs to thrive is to be connected to the God who created it. Only then can we feel like our lives have a meaning and purpose that transcends merely "showing up" every day. But to find this holy connection we have to be moored to our Great Faith, which is so much sturdier than my little spirituality. We need a faith inherited from thousands of years of prophets, apostles, martyrs, theologians, and nameless ordinary people who've already faced everything in life we possibly could but who stood up in worship every Sunday to say, "I believe . . ."

Not only does this Great Faith give us a sturdy inheritance that was hammered out on the anvil of adversity, it also catches us up in a better story than we can possibly script for ourselves. The point of worship is not to make the inherited tradition relevant to me, but to make me relevant to the high drama of God's work in the world. The tradition claims that my life began not when I graduated from college, got married, got a job, or a better job, or finally figured out how to retire. It didn't even begin when I was born. According to the opening words of the Bible, life starts with the words, "In the beginning, God . . ." And according to the end of the book, it ends with a holy vision of God being at home among mortals, a river of life, and a tree with leaves for the healing of the nations. Everything in between is more the unfolding of this sacred dream. And since we get to participate in that, we're always moored to a story worthy of our fleeting years.

Of course, there are things in the creed and certainly in the Christian tradition that give us problems. Anyone who doesn't have serious questions about the church hasn't read much history. Or paid attention to the failings of every congregation. But even our objections require a tether to something worth rebelling against. Along the way the questions shape the tradition, which is always evolving, but they also shape our souls and make them weighty and strong. It is both the comfort of the tradition and the struggle against it that leaves the soul with gravitas.

Sadly, this was all a bridge too far for Jeff. He left my office discouraged because he couldn't get over the priority of his own faith over our Great Faith. I understand this. Nothing is more countercultural today than saying the Apostles' Creed. In a society that now prefers personal mission statements to old confessions of faith it sounds crazy to inherit beliefs. But one of the great things about the tradition is that it's waiting for us when we're ready to come home.

Frantically Preparing for the Prince of Peace

I know we're all supposed to love Advent, but I find its approach to be mostly demanding. This hardly distinguishes me as a pastor. Most of my parishioners see this month as a season of incredible expectations. There are parties to plan, travel arrangements to make, presents to buy/wrap/mail, a tree and a house to decorate, and Christmas cards to produce that present a glowing photograph of the family and a brief message about the wonders of the last year concluding with something spiritual like "Come, Lord Jesus, Prince of Peace." Every year it's the same routine—we frantically prepare the way for peace.

As a pastor, the demand I feel most acutely is the congregation's expectation that I'll show up in the pulpit with something new and inspiring to say about Mary, Joseph, and their baby. But the subtext of this expectation is the yearnings we have about our own families at this holiday.

During the coffee hour after worship today Jenny Adams told me that she would be going back to Indiana in a couple of weeks to be with her family. With a roll of her eyes she added that her mother had purchased matching Christmas sweaters for everyone. That's not even subtext. That's a clear declaration of her mother's dressed-up dream for the family. But this is the same family she had last year, and all the years before that, so her dreams are in serious trouble. And when the congregation looks beyond its own yearnings to again encounter the angel's proclamation of "peace on earth," the gospel never seems more out of touch with current events than at this time of year.

But every Advent something climbs up from our souls that is asking for a Christmas gift from God. My job is to see that, to honor it, and to gently reveal how the hopes and fears of all the years are met in the coming of the Savior. "Come, Lord Jesus, Prince of Peace."

There are only four chapters of the Gospels that describe the nativity. After all these years, and after all the Advent sermons the congregation has already heard, I wonder what new insight is left to reveal. I have a strong hunch those in the pews are wondering the same thing.

The right response to this familiar preacher's lament, I know, is to claim that my task is not to be new and creative but just to present the gospel. But that's not what the congregation is thinking. I see them sitting in the pews with their arms crossed daring me to say anything about the Christmas miracle that hasn't been so well trodden that it's stomped down any trace of miracle left in the text.

We have a biblical archaeologist on the faculty of the seminary where I often teach a course. More than once I've suggested to him that if he could discover a new character for the nativity narratives of the Bible I could finish my career. But he keeps saying he's got nothing else. I'm stuck with the text as it is.

The text stands unchanged before the pastor. After all the workshops, lectionary study groups, scholarly commentaries, and op-ed columns we've scavenged, we are still left with the same biblical text to which the church has been bound for over two thousand years. If we are going to say anything worth hearing to those who are still hopeful enough to trudge into church hoping that a savior may actually come this Advent, it has to come from these same four chapters of the Bible.

The Christmas miracle for me is that every time I approach these same texts there is always something there, lying just beneath the surface, that I've never seen before. I've learned the hard way to trust this. Every Advent begins with doubt and mental anxieties that the elders will call a special meeting to discuss the problem of the pastor being dried up. But after hard hours in The Study excavating these all-too-familiar four chapters, it ends with me smiling in humble gratitude, surprised that there was so much more in the text than I knew. And then I can't wait to get to the pulpit.

So many things have formed my soul over the long years of this calling, but nothing has shaped me more than the biblical text. Every time I dare to think I am too familiar with it, I'm humbled by the discovery that I am still in a third-grade Sunday school class learning the holy stories and mysteries for the first time.

Precisely because it is the gospel, the text wants to surprise me. I just have to shuffle off the heavy cloak of being a professional with too many academic degrees to see it again as wide-eyed as a child on Christmas morning. "A baby who is God with us? Really?"

If I am not surprised by the miracle, the chances are beyond great that no one who shows up on Christmas Eve will be either. They at least need to believe that I believe in the miracle. I have to believe it so much that I'm willing to stand up in front of everyone and say, "Look at this! Look! Can you believe it?" Or as the first messengers of God said, "Behold! I bring you good news of great joy."

This is my real burden every Advent. How do I get involved in all of my own family's manic preoccupations with the holiday and still "go and search diligently for the child"? If I say that I have a higher calling than getting frantic about the upcoming party at the house, then I am not faithful to my even higher calling of being a partner to my spouse who is knocking herself out on a dinner to which mostly church people will come. But if I wander away from The Study too long to work on the holiday, I'm not going to be able to find the miracle of the holy day that is wrapped in those four chapters.

I think Jesus knows this all too well. After all, he came to a couple that was probably more worried about finding a place to spend the night than giving birth to the salvation of the world. And maybe that's the way God's hope is supposed to show up—as a Christmas surprise that quietly pierces through our anxious plans, offering more hope than we can see today because, frankly, we're too busy celebrating it. But this newborn hope will grow into our salvation. "Come, Lord Jesus, Prince of Peace."

Week Three

A Young Pastor in Deep Waters

Forty-three years ago, I had just been ordained as an assistant pastor when I received a phone call from Mr. Jenkins, a trustee of the congregation, asking me to visit him at his home. I assumed he wanted to get to know the new youth pastor at his congregation. I had just turned twenty-six years old and graduated from seminary only a month earlier.

When I arrived at the house, I discovered that I was actually meeting with Mr. and Mrs. Jenkins, their eighteen-year-old son Todd, his seventeen-year-old girlfriend Jennifer, and her mother Mrs. Enright. I walked in the door to find them all sitting in the living room that was clearly filled with tension. Todd and Jennifer were holding hands looking down at the floor. Mrs. Jenkins was wiping away tears.

As soon as I sat in my assigned seat, Mr. Thompson said, "Reverend, I'm sure you're busy so I'll get right to the point. Our son has got this young lady pregnant. We have all talked about this, and we've decided the kids should get married. They're obviously very young, but we'll all help raise this baby. The details have all been worked out. All we really need to know is if you'll perform this wedding. I'm sure you will want to . . ."

Mrs. Enright angrily interrupted: "We have not all agreed! That is just your opinion. I think this idea of a baby is a mistake, and Jenny shouldn't even be carrying it still. Pastor, tell him that these kids shouldn't wreck their lives over a youthful indiscretion."

I will never forget a word of this staggering conversation. I want to believe I immediately entered into an internal prayer while I started to respond to this family, but I'm not sure I knew how to do that in those days. I do remember asking Todd and Jennifer how they were feeling about this, and I remember the very long silence that followed.

Eventually Todd said, "I don't know what I'm feeling. I just want to do the right thing." Then for the first time Jennifer looked up from the floor and asked me, "What do you think we should do?" There was another long silence.

I didn't realize it at the time, but this was when I began to learn about the need for pastors to develop skills in digging around to discover subtext. My seminary taught me a great deal about how to exegete the Bible and the Christian tradition, but nothing about how to exegete the congregation I had just vowed to serve with "energy, intelligence, imagination, and love."

It is now clear to me that there were so many dynamics lying beneath this tense moment in the Jenkinses' living room. Certainly there were more than I could know, but I should have started asking myself some of these questions:

Why did Mr. Jenkins ask the rookie pastor to handle this complex pastoral concern?

What did it say about the Jenkins family dynamic that the father was running the show?

Why wasn't Mrs. Jenkins saying anything?

What was the nature of Mrs. Enright's relationship with Jennifer?

Was there a Mr. Enright? And what did it mean if there wasn't?

Who were Todd and Jennifer, and what was their maturity level?

Why did Mr. Jenkins insist that this incredibly young couple marry and have the baby?

Why did Mrs. Enright not want that just as desperately?

How would we make our way through the complex issue of abortion, or adoption, or a young marriage?

And most importantly, what was going on here theologically?

At least I stumbled into the right strategy of slowing down the conversation. I made it clear to them that while I understood they were concerned about making a decision, we did have a little time to sort through the complicated choices before them with some care. This didn't make Mr. Jenkins very happy with me, and I assumed he would soon be on the phone with the senior pastor about his disappointment. But it did seem to provide some relief to Todd and Jennifer.

What followed was a series of conversations between me and the senior pastor; between me and Todd and Jennifer alone; between Todd and Jennifer and a counselor I found; and between me and the parents. After several weeks of this, a lot of answers to questions I didn't even know to ask started to come to the surface.

In the end, I told Todd and Jennifer that as their pastor I would do the wedding if that is what they wanted and if Jennifer, as a minor, had her mother's permission. But I told them that regardless of their decision about the baby, I thought that getting married was a mistake. Then I backed up to let them make their choice, knowing I would stay with them regardless of what it was. I never would have come to that position without the help of the senior pastor who, by the way, refused to step in and take this mess off my hands in spite of my pleading.

It's striking to me that my pastoral ministry began with those three incredibly thick weeks. I didn't sleep much in those days, and I found that I was constantly brooding over the intense family dynamics into which I had been tossed. But as I look back on that experience now I realize there was also something intense forming in me.

My own soul was beginning its transformation into that of a pastor's. It wasn't exactly a painful change, but it did turn a lot of things upside down in me. As one who had spent a lot of years in school, I had to learn there was no way I was going to get an A on this. Those days were forever gone. I also had to discover that if I tried to move this in a particular direction, I would essentially turn into either Mr. Jenkins or Mrs. Enright, and I knew I was called to something holier in their lives than being right. But this was the first time in my young life that being right was not the right thing to be. It was actually beside the point of my calling. However, I did eventually develop a conviction about their situation that would have been dishonest not to offer as a pastor.

Perhaps most importantly, I was just beginning to learn how to bring messiness into my own soul that used to be tidy and uncrowded. This teen pregnancy, and all the complicating family dynamics swirling around it, was not a puzzle to be figured out in my mind. It was a pathos that I was called to bring into my deepest encounters with God. My brooding had to turn into prayer. My confusion had to become humility. My theology had to be pushed through real-life drama. My nature to be careful could not prevent me from eventually taking a position. And a parishioner's efforts to manipulate me meant I had to learn how to disappoint people who would be very unhappy with me.

Of course, little of this occurred to me at the time. I was mostly just reacting the best I could as I tried to find as much help as possible. But I've thought about those first three weeks of my ministry often over the last forty-three years. It was where something started that has continued to transform my soul through all the circling years of my ministry.

I only wish that somehow I could travel back in time to have a conversation with that twenty-six-year-old rookie pastor, to reassure him that while this is only the beginning of pastoral formation in him, and while it certainly isn't going to get any easier, he will find that opening his soul to human messiness is a way of encountering holiness. And even though he'll never get used to it, he will come to love it.

All this came back to me tonight after I got home from a disastrous committee meeting and began to flip through the new Christmas cards Ellie had left on the kitchen table. Like every year, I found the one from Todd and Jennifer that contained a family picture with their twins and several squirming grandchildren.

I was wrong in my considered conviction that their marriage would never last. Right. That happens a lot.

A Wedding for the Nonbeliever

Cyndi Parker and her fiancé Skip Jordan came to see me at the church earlier this week. They both live in San Jose, where they met, but want to get married in June at our church. They are both here for the Christmas holidays visiting Cyndi's extended family and introducing Skip to them. This was a convenient time to meet with me about their plans for the wedding.

Cyndi and her family have been part of the congregation for several generations. She was very involved in our children and youth programs, but she hasn't been attending any church since leaving for college ten years ago. When I asked her about this, she said, "I just couldn't find another church like St. Andrews." (She actually thinks that's an impressive argument for not worshiping in San Jose.) Then she assured me that she's never left the faith and can't imagine getting married anywhere but at her home church.

I left that alone for a while and asked Skip what he thought about this idea. He shrugged and said, "It's okay with me because I know it's really important to Cyndi." Pastor that I am, I asked, "Is it important to you?" He responded with, "To tell you the truth, not really. If it was up to me, we would get married by a friend on the beach. But as long as her parents are footing the bill for this thing, I don't care. Just so long as it isn't real religious because, no offense Reverend, I don't believe all that stuff."

"I see," I said as flatly as possible. "You realize, Skip, that in our tradition weddings are worship services. The liturgy is clearly Christian. I can't pull Jesus Christ out of your wedding."

The temperature in the room was starting to rise when Skip shot back, "Look, my family and all my friends know I'm an atheist. I would feel like a hypocrite looking religious all of a sudden at my wedding."

"I understand," I responded, again flatly. "I don't want you to be a hypocrite either. But I'm a pastor and can only officiate at a wedding that claims you're making a holy covenant."

By now Cyndi was crying. A lot. She blurted out. "Can't the two of you work this out? St. Andrews is my church. I have always dreamed of being married here because it would be so perfect. My grandmother is Thelma Parker, who's been an elder here like forever. Pastor, I just can't believe you're going to wreck my wedding on a technicality."

I've been here before. Often. A daughter of the church takes a break from worshiping when she moves away, but not from her heritage of faith. She meets a guy, falls in love, and plans to implement her childhood dream of someday walking down the aisle of this sanctuary where she probably once starred as Mary in the Christmas pageant. Only the guy she wants to marry is not a believer. But since she loves him so much, she can't bring herself to confront the huge issue of believing in a God he thinks doesn't exist. So she waits until they meet with the minister for me to "work this out" with him. When it isn't working out, she pulls out the "my grandmother is an elder" card. As if that's not enough, she tearfully begs me not to wreck her wedding on a technicality like not being able to pull God out of the ceremony.

Cyndi wants to make the conflict between me and Skip, or even between me and her family who she believes has a right to have a wedding in the sanctuary. I have to be careful not to take my assigned role in this drama she has written. I'm not really the source of the conflict. Not this time.

So I said to Cyndi and Skip, "Here's what I can do. I will give you a copy of the wedding liturgy today. You take it back to San Jose and read it carefully. We can make some adjustments to it like substituting one Scripture text for another, but you're going to find that it's a very Christian liturgy. It has prayers like, 'It is only by receiving your grace in Jesus Christ, O God, that we know how to offer grace in the holy bonds of matrimony.' We're stuck with the lines that are like that. If after carefully reviewing this liturgy, you decide you still want me to officiate at the wedding, then I will gladly do it."

Now the decision is in their court. Should Cyndi's parents want to talk to me about this wedding, and I'll be stunned if they don't, I don't have to say that I refused to do the wedding. I offered to officiate at a worship service that blessed their vows, if that's what they want. But that's just good church politics.

More importantly, it is not my integrity that is on the line should this very Christian wedding happen in the sanctuary. It's really Skip who has to choose between making his wife happy and being a hypocrite. That's a choice the two of them should have been talking about long before they came to see me. And this issue runs a lot deeper than their wedding. They may be able to work it out, but not without talking about it. A lot.

The annual Christmas card from Todd and Jennifer Jenkins has become my Advent angel reminding me to step out of the role that takes responsibility for who should or should not be getting married. But as the pastor, it is my role to confront couples with their own responsibility for making this commitment, and their responsibility for deciding what they're going to do about God in their marriage.

When Cyndi and Skip left my office, it was not clear what they would do. It is clear that their conversation with me didn't go as they had hoped. And I'm pretty sure my conversation with Cyndi's parents won't go as I hope.

Christmas Eve

Being Joseph in the Pageant

Tonight the children's ministry presented their annual Christmas pageant. When it started, I found myself counting up how many Marys I have later married, how many Baby Jesuses I have watched grow up into everything but the Savior, and how many young Herods turned out to be cast exactly right. But long ago my favorite character in the pageant became Joseph.

He has no lines in the drama, although some years he pantomimes asking the innkeeper for a room only to turn back to Mary looking like a failure. When I was a child participating in these pageants none of us wanted to be Joseph. He's not the star. This year the director of the pageant once again convinced another tall, awkward preadolescent boy to take the part. And once again Joseph spent most of his time standing behind the beatific Mary and her baby looking like he didn't really want to be there.

This is pretty much true of the original Joseph as well. He only shows up three times in the Gospels, and he never speaks. The way Matthew's Gospel tells the story, Joseph doesn't even want as much attention as he gets. He had other plans. He just wanted to marry his Mary, pay his taxes, and settle down to a quiet life as a carpenter. But all that had to change when Mary became pregnant. God interrupted Mary's life, and as a result Joseph was never the same.

The best he got from heaven was a dream that this was going to turn out really well. But since the dream told him not to "put Mary away" even quietly, everyone in town was going to assume this must be his baby and that they couldn't wait until they were married to sleep together. So he has to share in the scandal that was never his idea.

By the time Joseph learns about this miracle of the incarnation being formed in Mary's womb, all of the decisions have been made and the process is well underway. The angel didn't say, "Here's what we're thinking Joseph—the birth of a Savior! We were thinking about using your fiancée's womb, but we wanted to run the idea by you." No, the way the story goes, Joseph is mostly just trying to keep up with the next strange chapter.

It's interesting that the director of the pageant never has trouble finding a girl who wants to be Mary. In fact, it's actually rather competitive. And the cool guys tend to vie for one of the wise men roles. But this year as I prepare the Christmas Eve homily, I'm wondering what if the key to the whole story is Joseph? What if none of us are supposed to be the star of the drama? And unlike the shepherds, we can't just go back to the sheep after beholding the child on this holy night. What if the Christmas angels are trying to tell us that the life we were expecting is not what we're going to live, but this is actually for our salvation? And if we read ahead a bit in the drama, we'll discover that like Joseph we should settle into being confused and out of the loop when God is making decisions.

And what if I had a clue about how to make that sound like "joy to the world" in the Christmas Eve homily?

Maybe the starting point is realizing that I too am the awkward Joseph. I didn't write the pageant. But I've been a pastor long enough to know that most of us are worn out on our own plans for life. And we're ready to hear about a more interesting story than we can write for ourselves even if we don't really understand it. Somehow I need to communicate that that's always been the dream at Christmas. And maybe it is high time for the church to get back to taking responsibility for the world's scandals because that really would bring joy to the world.

This is not my first Christmas Eve homily, but it will probably be my last. I find it striking that in the end I'm focusing on not being the star of the drama. The confusing dream that outlives us is really all we need.

January

The Long, Gray Days of Ministry

This is such a gray month. Most people in the parish are recovering from their last failed effort at creating the perfect family holiday. Apparently, buying everyone matching Christmas sweaters and singing by the piano didn't work out as planned at Jenny Adams's family home in Indiana. Similarly, I'm fretting over what we should have done differently in the Advent worship services—as if I could have pulled down the second coming of Christ to St. Andrews Presbyterian Church with a better liturgy. Our family's once beautifully adorned Christmas tree is now stripped bare and lying by the curb with what few needles remain on it. And the morning radio just announced a sleet storm that's closed down the interstate. So what happened to "joy to the world"?

Those who don't hang around churches make New Year's Eve parties their great hope for a better year. But that doesn't work out any better than Advent does for the church. January just keeps returning as though the angel's message was "cold, gray news for all the people."

A long time ago the historic church began to celebrate Epiphany in January, which celebrates the later arrival of the magi to Bethlehem. I've long thought of that as a desperate effort at an encore for the hopes at Christmas. Epiphany has never really caught on with the congregation, and I think that's because we feel in our bones that January is the month for sighing.

It makes me wonder about what Mary and Joseph did after the shepherds left the manger. My hunch is they looked at each other, "pondering all these things," shrugged, and then shuffled back to doing what they had to do to make life work.

But I can still see the little girl on the third pew, right-hand side, whose face was aglow from the candle she held on Christmas Eve as we sang "Silent Night." She was thinking something miraculous was happening. Maybe she was on to something, and more was happening than we saw. Maybe after all these years the Savior still prefers to show up like he did in Bethlehem—so quietly that most people miss it.

It's not so hard to see that on Christmas Eve. My job is to help us all see it on a gray January Sunday after the poinsettias have died, the choir has tucked away its music for Handel's *Messiah*, and we've all returned to a sanctuary that looks like a barn the day after the shepherds went home.

What's fascinating is that people still come back to church in January. But where else would they go? This is where we celebrate our high holy days, where we listen for the still small voice on the gray ones, and where we ponder all these things in front of the God who created all the months.

The Obituary Writer

Jerry Pappas is a seventy-something-year-old member of the congregation. He and his wife Sophie are also members of the Greek Orthodox church in town because being Orthodox is an integral part of their Greek identities. But they're in our pews almost every Sunday, and they're the kind of couple that is always serving the food and busing tables at our congregational dinners.

In spite of his age, Jerry continues to work full time as the obituary writer for the city paper, a job he loves. He looks like a newspaperman—his white hair is a bit too long, his glasses are smudged, and he always wears the same tattered navy blazer with papers sticking out of the side pockets. But when he shakes your hand he has a gentle smile that just makes your day.

About every two months Jerry invites me to have lunch with him at Zorbas, the local Greek diner. It's a bit of a greasy spoon that has achieved iconic status in our town. The place is always full of blue-collar workers, students, and executives in expensive suits who love eating at a joint where the waitresses ask, "What'll it be?" If you really need an omelet and bad coffee at two o'clock in the morning, Zorbas is your place. Jerry grew up with the owner of the diner, whom he introduces to me at every lunch. He loves this diner and everything it represents.

I enjoy my lunches with Jerry because I get to probe his work, which is quite close to mine. When he's assigned to write an obit, the first thing he does is make an appointment to meet with the family. Over coffee in the kitchen he interviews them to find out all he can about the deceased as a person. What he's trying to discover is the passion, the core experiences, or whatever it is that merits being the final words on this person's life. Jerry is essentially writing secular eulogies.

When he was a young man he paid his way through college by working as a waiter at an exclusive private club downtown. During those years he got to know many of the powerful and wealthy captains of industry in our town who let down their guard around him because he was just a waiter. Since he was so much younger than these giants of the city, he's outlived all of them. And now he's writing their obituaries. So the waiter ended up publishing the last words on the leaders of the community.

Every lunch with Jerry is like listening to a Greek comedy play. I keep hearing about someone who came from nowhere, worked hard, took advantage of the bizarre twists of fate, and ended up as a demigod. The vast majority of his obituaries, which are about people who were relatively unknown, follow the same pattern as those who died on top of the world. I keep waiting for the Greek tragedy play where someone who started out on top fell to the bottom. But Jerry doesn't care for tragedy plays. He told me that if he dug deep enough he could find the redemption in anyone.

Like I said, his job is quite close to mine.

Week Three

The Pastoral Search Committee

I got a call today from a pastoral search committee of a large congregation. They were checking the reference of a pastor named Jeff Bantam, who used to be our associate at St. Andrews before he struck out on his own as a solo pastor. Jeff came to us right out of seminary, did a good job here, and as far as I've heard he's had a good experience for the last five years in his congregation. I'm not surprised that's he moving up to a larger church. He's talented, charismatic, a great preacher, and ambitious without being arrogant. He's also thirty-five, which seems to be the preferred age these days for new senior pastors.

I've been a bit dismayed by how many of the pulpits in the larger congregations are now filled with pastors who are Jeff's age. When asked to recommend names to a search committee, I often extol the benefits of hiring the fifty-something veteran pastors who've already learned from their youthful mistakes and have developed some important insights about the soul of a congregation. But I've never been convincing. They won't say it, but most of these search committees have their hearts set on hiring a rising star. When I was complaining about this to Ellie she asked, "Isn't Jeff about the age you were when we came here?"

When I think back on all the big mistakes I made as a pastor in my thirties, probably the greatest one was wanting to be a rising star. I never would have admitted that was my agenda, even to myself, but in those days hubris was a silent partner in most of my decisions. Another advantage to being a veteran of this work is that after four decades the churches I served have kicked most of that out of me. It's another way congregations help the spiritual lives of their pastors. I don't think anyone ever thought much about it or had a plan to put me in my place. They just let me fail enough times for me to get the message myself. And they let me discover that the success of the all-so-important new programs I initiated didn't really make that much difference to anyone, including me. All that fuss only left us busier and more tired. But the most important way the congregation helped me stop thinking about my future is that it kept me distracted with the far more compelling stories of our parishioners' lives.

I can still remember the youthful flutter in my heart every time I received a call from a search committee. Only in those days I wasn't being asked to give a recommendation; I was the one who had been recommended to the committee. I couldn't wait to get home, tell my wife, and maybe a friend or two, all as a way of dwelling on the possibility of moving up to a new life. This was before every church had a website, so I would have to wait for the search committee to mail me a packet of information on their congregation. The day that package arrived I would pore over the bulletins and annual reports like I was salivating over travel brochures for Paris. I couldn't get enough of the thought that maybe my best life was at a different, and thus wonderful, church where I would really be appreciated.

When I came to this church at age thirty-nine from the place I'd previously been serving, I was sure I was moving up in my career. It was a larger congregation, but it didn't take me long to realize I hadn't actually moved up as much as over. It was remarkable how little really changed when I came here. The rhythms of worship, committee meetings that go on forever and accomplish little, the ubiquitous potlucks, the problem of the dysfunctional secretary everyone's afraid to fire, and the frantic effort to fight through city traffic to make a hospital visit only to discover that the patient was just discharged, were all the same. And I soon found every grumpy, pain-in-the-neck parishioner I thought I'd left in the last congregation front and center in the new one. Different names and faces, but the exact same people. There is no moving up out of any of that. Nor should there be.

Along the way, through all those early dreams of escaping, I eventually woke up to the discovery that I was constantly bumping into human souls. And if I would let them, they would tell me the most amazing things about their lives. Most of them who had stories of hurt knew I couldn't fix anything for them, but they wanted their pastor to know and to talk to God about them. Those who had dreams, joys, and major life events wanted me there to hold the new baby, bless the marriage, or give thanks for the new job. The new widow would walk into the sanctuary for the funeral holding my arm and squeezing it tightly. With every one of those stories, my own story slowly changed over the years because I fell in love with these people.

As in any mature relationship, the way you express love often is by doing the dishes, paying the bills, doing the laundry. It doesn't matter if you have a gift for it; what matters is how you do it. When it's done as an expression of love, it's a lot more enjoyable. I eventually stopped complaining about the complainers, found ways of making committee meetings more enjoyable even if I was just entertaining myself, and stopped rolling my eyes when the elders fell back into their same old debates about whether a special offering would detract from the general offering. Because if I didn't do all of that ordinary stuff with authentic love, they weren't going to call me when the baby was born or the husband died.

When I was an ambitious young associate pastor, the senior pastor of that congregation had a pretty light hand as a supervisor. I think that's because he knew the lessons I really needed to learn were only going to come from the congregation over many years. When I told him I had accepted a new call, he took me out to lunch. The only thing I remember about that conversation was when he said, "I've served three congregations over my ministry. And nothing worth anything happened until I surrendered to the congregation." This was so bizarre to me I had no idea even how to ask him a question about what he meant. *Why would a leader surrender?* I wondered. He saw my confusion, graciously smiled, and changed the subject.

Now I get it. I think. My old boss was not telling me to avoid dreams or holy visions for the congregation. He was just telling me to love the congregation God gave me more than my dreams for them. That was certainly the turning point in my ministry here. All the good things in the church came after I surrendered my heart to it. And precious few of those things were my ideas. Nor can I tell you whose ideas they were. They just rose up out of the creative space created by a pastor and congregation settling down with each other.

If I get a chance to talk to Jeff Bantam before he heads off to his bright future, I'm pretty sure I'm going to say something about the blessing of surrendering to his new congregation. He won't understand what I'm talking about any more than I did when I was his age. But if he's ambitious to love, he'll learn. And then some pretty exciting things will start to unfold from heaven.

Announcing the Retirement

Tonight, at the end of the monthly church elders meeting, I announced that at the end of June I would be retiring. Ironically, on the meeting agenda it came up under the topic "Unfinished Business." I avoided pressing the metaphor.

I was initially surprised that no one was surprised. Now, a couple of hours later, I'm surprised that I was surprised by how well they took it. They had to know this was coming sometime soon. The timing is right, the church is more than ready, and I should be ready as well. I can now banish my little fantasy that upon hearing the news the elders will rend their robes in anguish. Instead, what I saw around the meeting table was gentle smiles, nods of understanding, a couple of tears, and lots of congratulations.

My letter to the congregation has already been prepared, and it will go out in the morning. I pored over the writing of it for weeks. It now reminds me of the mistake that engaged couples make when they try to write their own wedding vows. Either their new, oh-so-personal, sort-of vows just sound goofy, or after repeated rewrites they produce something that sounds remarkably close to the traditional vows. I went with the second option. After all that work, my letter to the congregation sounds like something

I could have taken off the internet. And why should this surprise me either? I'm not the first pastor to retire, and there are only so many ways to make such an unremarkable announcement.

I think this should be the tone of the next six months of my ministry: "This is not remarkable. Nothing to see here. Please keep moving." I would actually find that comforting and reassuring. It would mean that the church is as ready as I think it is, and apparently as ready as the elders are, judging from tonight's meeting. The reality, of course, is that the congregation would handle it if I left after serving it for two years. So let's keep that sobriety about us in the months ahead.

The only action the elders took tonight was to appoint a planning committee to pull together a "Retirement Celebration," which is another sign of a board that was not stunned by my carefully prepared announcement. I responded by asking them if we could avoid making this a celebration of my ministry. I told them that instead I would love it if we would just have another potluck dinner in the fellowship hall, like so many we've enjoyed as a church family over the years. I said there could be a time for saying some goodbyes, maybe singing a hymn or two, and then we would have some good closure on this relationship. No one stood to sing the doxology at this suggestion, but they got my point. I think.

I find myself breathing easier tonight. There have been so many times when I thought something coming before the congregation would be easy when it was actually tumultuous, and times when I was prepared for a storm that never made it to shore. It's great that this retirement is going to be easier on the congregation than I feared.

I'm relieved, and yet a bit sad. A little storm would have been nice.

Listening to a Friend

James Kairns and I met for our normal monthly breakfast this morning. But this time the conversation wasn't normal.

James is the pastor of Fountain of Life Church, which is one of the leading Black congregations in our city. He and I met five years ago at a community development fundraiser. For reasons that aren't clear to either of us, we immediately became friends. He's a good bit younger than me, but very much my peer.

Our churches have worked together on several urban projects, including a tutoring program that promises to send kids to college. He's a Pentecostal and I'm a Presbyterian. When our churches worship together, his congregation tones it down a little and we key it up as high as we can go. Somehow the Holy Spirit makes it work.

I've always enjoyed our conversations at the local Perkins restaurant. Sometimes we talk about the city or our congregations, but other times we bat around stuff about our own lives. We've been to each other's homes for dinners and birthday parties. I was at the hospital when his wife had a devastating late-term miscarriage a few years back. We know each other really well, or so I thought.

Last night James was pulled over by a policewoman while driving home from a church dinner. His wife and six-year-old daughter

143

were in the car. There was no reason for the stop other than that he was driving a nice car in a rough neighborhood—his neighborhood. She checked his driver's license and registration while the three of them sat in the car with a brilliant light from the police cruiser flooding their car. Assured that he was a good citizen, the policewoman gave him back his documents and told him to be careful in this part of town.

"Do you have any idea how many times this has happened to me?" James asked. My eyes dropped into my lap. He said several other things that culminated in, "You'll never be able to understand what it's like to be a Black man in our society." I nodded my agreement but didn't know what to do with the chasm I suddenly felt between us, the one that James had probably always seen.

Then he told me that the last time he preached at my congregation, one of our smiling parishioners shook his hand at the door following worship and said, "We're always so happy to have you speak to us because you're not angry." I was horrified that our congregation would accept a Black preacher but only if that Black preacher were not angry. Staring me in the eye he said, "I am angry. And it's high time that your church knows that there's plenty to be angry about."

I agreed and asked him to come back to a worship service and speak about this righteous anger. James just pushed his coffee cup away, paused, and whispered, "Yeah . . . sure."

It's not as though James and I had avoided race while working together in the community. But apparently we've been using White rules to talk about it. Our church doesn't really know what to do with anger. We even have a Book of Order that's designed to regulate all of the emotion out of the church. It's easier for us to work on "the race issue" than to see the humiliation of those who are beaten down by social injustice. But when you're pulled over in your own neighborhood because you're driving a car that's too nice, you're dealing with more than an issue. You're fighting for your dignity.

The typical accusation against the White church is that it likes to have conversations about race but it's not doing much. Ironically, our church has spent years hard at work beside an African American church, but clearly we haven't been listening to them very well.

Through all these years that our congregation has worked with the Black Pentecostals in the community, and for all the years James and I have been friends, we've avoided discussing the deep personal hurts caused by racism. I've spent all day wondering about that. I'm now thinking it's not only because we don't know how to handle anger but maybe also because James and his church don't want to be stigmatized as angry Black folk. But as he says, there's plenty to be angry about. And if we're really going to be friends it's high time to dive into this.

I have no idea how it's going to be received at our congregation when we move into this deeper truth-telling. And I wonder what James and I will do about the chasm between us that I failed to see amid all those birthday parties we shared. It was rough this morning, and yet I'm pretty sure James has a lot more truth to offer.

Somehow the Holy Spirit will make it work. Otherwise all those lovely joint worship services were just distant brothers and sisters trying to play nice.

February

Making Sense of a Pastor's Cancer

Today I had my third round of radiation treatment for the melanoma. It burns a good bit and leaves me off-kilter, but at least it's not chemotherapy. The more tests they've run, the better the news. Even the surgery was a relatively minor one-day event. We're blessed to live in a city with wonderful medical care. I'm not out of the woods by any means, but I'm on a path that has a good chance of getting me there. For that I'm overwhelmingly grateful. Hope is a precious gift. I'm also grateful that neither the disease nor the treatments have prevented me from working full tilt.

Now that the future of my health is looking more hopeful, it's been easier to ponder what this means. There is certainly the Joe Lincoln school of thought that it's just another illustration that we aren't in control of our lives, and life is a humility from beginning to end. I find that compelling. My doctors prefer to think of the disease as something evil, although they don't use that word. They don't want to manage the evil, they want to cast it out. And I am certainly all for that. Ellie and Mackenzie both think of it as the bogeyman in the night, again not their words. But they speak about the cancer mostly in terms of fear, even a terrifying threat that doesn't belong in our home. Father

Ted talks about it mostly as a call to worship even if it's not a very pretty liturgy.

For me, it has become all of these things, but on any given day I could be closer to one of these thoughts than another. As I've continued reading the psalms through these last few months, even early on when God and I weren't talking about it, I find they present a variety of responses: lament, petition, anger, hope, even gratitude. I figure that if the psalmists don't have to settle into one way of thinking about the threats to life, neither do I. On any given day I could have tried to write any of these psalms.

When James Kairns and I were talking about it at one of our recent breakfast meetings, he said that as a pastor he was wondering how having cancer affected my pastoral care. I told him that I've been wondering that too. I would love to say that it's given me more empathy for people with cancer, but there are so many types of cancer, and it's such a personal disease, that I'm not sure anyone who has it is really all that interested in empathy.

What everyone is always looking for is compassion, and I suppose having cancer is making me a better pastor in understanding both the yearnings and the limits of that search. I've drawn a tight circle around me of people who know about this disease, and I've now figured out that's because they're the only ones from whom I want compassion. A large circle of loving concern is more terrifying to me than the cancer. That's just the way I'm wired. I've had a couple of pastor friends who were flaming extroverts with cancer. Soon after they were diagnosed they got a page on the CaringBridge website, which allows anybody to receive updates or reflections on a person's condition. It's a wonderful tool. For extroverts.

Having this disease is reminding me that there is no one style of pastoral care that fits all people in any particular dilemma. I really have to know my parishioners and honor the way God uniquely wired them. I may have made some mistakes in putting people's names in the pastoral prayer in our Sunday worship services.

James and Father Ted both keep asking me if I'm going to tell St. Andrews about this. I love it that they know me well enough to ask "if" and not "when." The answer as of today is that I still don't know if I will tell them. They will be hurt if I don't, and I may be hurt if I do. Most of the time over the years I have chosen to take the hurt as an expression of love. But for some reason I haven't said anything to them about this, and it's been three months. It isn't that I love them any less. And I don't think it's because I am pulling away as I prepare to retire, because I'm clearly not doing that at work. However, if I weren't retiring I would certainly feel compelled to tell them so they could make alternative plans for a pastor just in case this thing goes south. So actually, the pending retirement has given me the luxury of pondering this question of disclosure.

Father Ted refers to this as my delicious pondering, and now he has me pondering why I am pondering. Sheesh.

A Wintry Funeral for Young Teddy

I was surprised by how few people were in the church for Teddy Thompson's funeral. Maybe it was the weather that made it hard for people to get there. The tender white snow that once blanketed us had become dirty gray after all the commuters had driven through it and the plows had pushed it aside. Piles of worn-out snow lined every slippery street. And then another storm.

Teddy was a well-known young adult who grew up in the church. I remember the year, long ago, that he was Joseph in our Christmas Eve pageant. At the end of the service that night we walked out of the sanctuary into a gentle, new snow still singing "silent night, holy night" while clutching our candles that provided such little light. Teddy and several other boys tried to put their candles together to make a bigger fire.

That was then. In recent years, Teddy's eyes became distant, flameless, and for almost ten years we were all worried about him. Then he shot himself in the head.

We had so much warning that he was slipping away, but no one could grab his hand. Teddy's mother had spoken with me about him several times, and with him and me a couple of times. I recommended a psychiatrist who Teddy went to see, but it wasn't at all evident that he was taking the medication that was prescribed. He had fallen into some place so deep not even an anxious mother could find him.

He used to have a frustrated girlfriend, but she told his mother she couldn't keep trying to break through to someone who was so severely depressed. She was young and had her whole life in front of her, she said, and needed a man who could love her back. Teddy's mother quickly gave her absolution, saying, "Of course. I understand."

He had so many Sunday school teachers and a youth group leader who used to meet with him at Starbucks. They were fabulous with him on the infrequent times he returned to church, and they joined others in the church in fretting about him, asking, "Is Teddy okay?"

"No," was all I could say.

He used to have friends, many who joined him on Youth Sunday when Teddy and the other high school seniors gave their testimony before the congregation. He did a great job speaking about how grateful he was to his mother for showing him the love of Jesus Christ, and how proud he was of her taking care of him and his younger brother after their father left. I remember the photo our church newsletter published showing the seniors on that morning with all of them arm on shoulder, smiling, even laughing, as if their future were only bright.

There is so much that "used to" describe Teddy.

His friends long ago left town to pursue their bright dreams. Teddy tried to do the same, but that's when the depression became acute, and he was dismissed before the end of his first year for missing too many classes. He moved back home to live with his mother. He tried a couple of dead-end jobs but couldn't hold any of them for long.

In our town there are mostly gray days in the winter, and you have to get your head around that to enjoy the place. But Teddy had become so gray he couldn't find the sun even on the days it was blasting through. Naturally, there would be another dark, sloppy storm at his funeral, and few would be able to get there even though his mother made it, of course. But all that was left was for her to weep on the first pew.

Even though I was Teddy's pastor and have known him his whole life, and saw this horrible tragedy coming but was unable to do anything to stop it, I don't actually feel guilt for not being able to prevent his suicide. This is not the first time I've watched this horrible tragedy unfold. I learned long ago that he was way beyond my reach but never beyond the reach of a Savior who knows all about dark places.

This is why eternity is so important to me. Our years on this earth are so fleeting, so easy to get wrong, and for some people the chemicals in their brain just take a self-destructive turn. There has to be a fuller life—one where we're not vulnerable to diseases and the life-draining hurts we inflict on each other and ourselves. And a place where the Christmas Eve snow never gets dirty and gray. Otherwise God was just a mad scientist running careless experiments with lab rats when he had the crazed idea of giving souls to humans. It cannot be that we were created only to yearn.

It wasn't hard for me to tell the small crowd that gathered in the dimly lit sanctuary, with the dingy snow and ice clinging to their boots, that Teddy was now in a place where there was no more despair. I still choose to believe in the Christmas Eve miracle where God is with us awkward Josephs, and we're with God, and the snow is gentle and unstained. The hard part is figuring out how to respond to his mother's broken heart.

I know that in the long days ahead she will keep pulling down the beautifully framed photo of the two of them that sits on the mantle of her living room, and the sadness will overwhelm her again and again. She may choose to blame his psychiatrist, girlfriend, or pastor. She'll certainly blame herself.

I have to resist the temptation of trying to take this anger from her. Blaming, doubting, wondering what if, is just part of the dark path she has to continue to take through the relentless storm called her grief. My job is simply to keep whispering to her that God knows, and nothing can separate her from the love she has for Teddy. The love she gets to keep.

The Blessed Church Lady

I try to visit our parishioners in the local nursing home on a regular basis, but to my embarrassment, if the church schedule gets demanding these visits are often the first thing to be postponed. But in the winter months, when the wind is biting cold, the folks who are shut in the nearby nursing home are always at the forefront of my mind.

Today I went to see Mrs. Thelma Parker. She's the grandmother of Cyndi Parker, who has decided to go with Skip's plan of getting married on the beach.

Mrs. Parker was once the queen of the congregation—always elegantly dressed, with a delicate smile. For twenty years she served as our clerk of session, which is probably the most influential lay office in our church. A big part of her job was to help the elders' various agendas gain some ground support in the congregation. That wasn't actually in her job description as the clerk, but she expanded the role. And she was really good at it.

In her heyday she made her way through the church's fellowship hall like a prima ballerina moving graciously, purposefully across the floor. Sometimes she provided a gentle non-anxious face on a small controversy that was being discussed by a few people. At other times she was welcoming a visitor, smoothing an elder's ruffled feathers from a difficult committee meeting, responding to a denominational vote that left someone grumpy, or answering questions about the new director of music. All the while she was sipping coffee and "just chatting."

She would hate the depiction, but she was a church politician with a string of pearls who knew how congregational democracies worked.

But she wasn't just an elegant worker bee. She loved our worship services, especially the music program. She was frequently the anonymous underwriter for the costs of special concerts, repairs on the organ, or the extra hymnbooks we needed. She liked her music classical and threatened that she would go into cardiac arrest if I let a guitar in the chancel. Of course, that meant I had to keep threatening to do just that someday.

Mrs. Parker, the name I always called her, embodied the best in the pastor-elder partnership. I will always be profoundly grateful for all she gave to the church and all she taught me along the way.

She had to stop being our clerk when she got too old to drive at night. For a while she continued to work the fellowship hall after worship on Sundays. Then her health declined even more, and she had to move into an assisted living facility. Six months ago she was transferred into the acute care rooms.

Now she is deep into her eighties and lying in the last room she will have on this earth. The days of butterflying her way through the halls of the church are long gone. Her declining health has ripped away all traces of her once regal countenance, and the old elegance is apparent only by the string of pearls she still wears. The deep lines on her always-powdered face lament her confusion over why she is still living.

I called for an appointment to see her. It's her way. Typically, before I arrive to visit her she would have coerced someone to do something about her hair. But this time my phone call was answered by a nurse who told me I should come as soon as possible.

Over my last couple of visits I discovered that dementia had begun to cloud her once sharp mind. The cancer has made its way through most of her body. And the hurting has now become so severe that her physician prescribed morphine—the last grace of medical caregivers who have abandoned hopes of curing.

When I arrived I found her foggy, struggling to find the old gifts of conversation. But she knows me, I think.

I told her all of the reassuring things that pastors say in this setting. "The Creator who has watched over you all of the days of your life, is now holding you in those sacred hands." She smiled and responded with words I didn't understand. I began to pray for her.

Then in a crystal-clear voice, with ease, she began to recite the words of old hymns: "Our God, Our Help in Ages Past," "Call Jehovah Thy Salvation," "A Mighty Fortress Is Our God," and of course "Amazing Grace." She even knew the second and third verses. I tried to say them along with her but dropped off because my memory failed long after she continued to make her declaration of faith through these historic lyrics of the church.

It is indeed an Amazing Grace that these old hymns have the power to break through the fog of morphine and dementia. She didn't quote anything from my sermons. In the end, nothing emerged from the often-repeated church vision statements, the building programs, great church battles, or the Bible studies she led for the women's association. Not even her many cherished relationships or family. In her last days it was only the old hymns that endured. *Through many dangers, toils, and snares, I have already come; 'Tis grace has brought me safe thus far, and grace will lead me home.*

I appreciate the validity of contemporary worship music. And I fully understand the value of praise choruses for those who find them more accessible than hymns. But I doubt that on a deathbed anyone will be singing "Our God Is an Awesome God." The problem with this popular song isn't the lyrics but its lack of gravitas. In the end Mrs. Parker needed to lean on something more sturdy.

Our slow demise on earth requires more than the little faith nurtured with thin melody lines that for some reason make you want to close your eyes as you sing. We need the eyes-wide-open great faith of the apostles, martyrs, mystics, reformers, and countless ordinary saints of the church. When an old servant of that church is dying, she needs the communion of saints cheering for her as she finishes the race. That is what the Scriptures, historic creeds, old hymns, and spirituals provide because they were all born out of heartache and suffering.

It's also what the last generation of church ladies are trying to offer us. They may not all die with great hymns on their lips, but the best of them were devoted to a faith that began before them and will outlive them.

Maybe there is something to the old formality, laced with tradition and graciousness, which is now out of style in worship. Beneath its tattered elegance a pastor sometimes finds a faith strong enough to carry us all the way home.

Taking the Heat for God

One of our high school seniors, Mary Jane Douglas, came to see me a few weeks ago. Her father, Stan, who's a trustee in the congregation, came along, which didn't surprise me since he was the one who made the appointment. Stan and I have long enjoyed a good relationship, and Mary Jane has been a marginally involved member of our youth group.

I baptized Mary Jane when she was held in Stan's arms as he stood next to his wife Jocelyn before the congregation. And I went to the emergency room the night a year later when Jocelyn didn't survive a horrible auto accident. Stan and I shared so many tears that night. I'll never forget standing at the graveside, trying to say something about the resurrection, watching him again holding his baby girl.

When the funeral was over Stan shook my hand and said, "Thank you." It was a long time ago, but I remember being puzzled by that response to all of the tears, prayers, and conversations we had about his wife's funeral. A handshake and "Thank you"? I didn't just bury his old Chevy. But anything more than "Thank you" would have cost too much.

Stan never remarried; he didn't even date as far as I know, although I watched more than one single woman in the church try to get his attention. He always hovered over Mary Jane as she grew up. Two years ago, he came to see me with a concern about our youth pastor, who he didn't think had the maturity for the job.

When I've had pastoral counseling appointments with a parent and child in the past, the parent usually takes over the long hour meeting trying to coax something out of the child, and hoping that when it finally spills out I'll be only too eager to help clean up the mess. I was expecting to hear a tortured confession from poor Mary Jane, and then see the imperatives in her father's eyes staring at me. But that's not what happened this time.

As soon as they sat on the sofa in my study, Mary Jane started to weep. Stan immediately put his arm around her and began to tear up as well.

What is it about a pastor's office that invites such vulnerability before any words are spoken? It isn't always tears that greet me. Sometimes the faces arrive red and the anger immediately spews. Other times people plop down on the sofa and lean way back as if there is simply no life left in the bodies that are too worn out to still hold them up. This time it was deep sorrow that walked in.

Stan was beyond speaking. After making two lunges toward my tissue box on the coffee table, young Mary Jane finally said, "I haven't been feeling very good for a while, so we went to our doctor. And then to a specialist, and then a whole bunch of tests. Turns out, I've got this horrible disease." At that point I was also on the verge of tears.

"Oh, Mary Jane," was all I could get out. While I was struggling to come up with something more helpful, she added, "It's going to get bad pretty fast." Then Stan managed to say, "This will paralyze her. By the time her prom comes around she'll be in a wheelchair."

What followed was mostly just all three of us taking turns at the tissue box.

I assured them of my own sorrow and that the congregation would do everything to surround them with compassion and any help we could provide, and that most importantly none of this was lost on the God who created Mary Jane and would never leave her. These are the things I was trained to say long ago. Then I prayed for her healing. I actually begged God, which is something I didn't learn in seminary.

When they left, I needed a pastor of my own, which is something else they didn't teach me in seminary. But a pastor didn't show up to help me be the pastor to Mary Jane and Stan. Instead the new chair of the property committee walked in as they walked out.

Really? What was I to do with the pathos that was all over my office while mentally saying, "Next"? And how was I now supposed to care about the new Christian education wing we were building? The transitions in this job give me soul whiplash.

I assumed that the tender pastoral moment with Mary Jane and Stan had bound us even closer together. And that the pastor's office had again become a confessional of brokenness, where I had been their faithful priest who may have fumbled a bit but who at least brought their heartache to the Healer. I thought we'd just begun another hard journey together. But yet again, that's not what happened.

What happened is that Mary Jane drew closer to our youth group, but not to me. And Stan dropped out of all his volunteer commitments at the church, worshiped sporadically on the back pew, and refused to look me in the eye when we passed in the church halls.

For almost a month I've tried to reach out to them. Mary Jane has been distant, and Stan has just assured me they're fine, and quickly hung up every time I've called. He's spoken to several elders about his doubts of my leadership. And of course, I can't explain this to anyone without betraying the confidentiality of our meeting.

Now I am left with my own thoughts to brood over what happened. In The Study at home, I've replayed in my mind that conversation in the office a hundred times over the last few weeks. I've discovered nothing. I wept with them, said nothing inappropriate other than offering painfully predictable reassurances, and I came up with a prayer that was at least sincere.

I have a theory that may be completely wrong, but it allows me to get to sleep at night while pondering their choice to wander away from my pastoral care. My hunch is based only on Stan's move to the back pew of the church in worship while Mary Jane remained tucked in beside her friends in the youth group who always sit in the balcony.

Every Sunday I stand before them in the pulpit wearing a black Geneva gown saying, "Hear the Word of the Lord."

Maybe their distance and anger has nothing to do with me. Maybe it has everything to do with my job to say a word from the Lord, who's the last person they want to speak to them. This was not their first crisis, but now it had become a crisis of faith.

Where are the miracles? This father and daughter had already been through so much, and yet they kept coming to church, standing for the doxology to sing "Praise God from whom all blessings flow." And now it sure looks like the blessings have run out.

Why?

I've been at this a long time and have buried too many people to be surprised by this question. But it still rattles around in my heart. For Mary Jane and Stan it's far more than a rattle.

So it falls to me to take the heat for their fury with God. Sometimes that's the best pastoral ministry I can offer.

March

The Weary Partisan

I've been reading George Orwell's book *Homage to Catalonia*, which describes his role in the Spanish Civil War. He doesn't attempt to provide objective history of the conflict but plainly states, "Everyone writes as a partisan."

When I was in college I missed this profound point and thought the debates were all about who has the truth. When I went to seminary, I learned to think the debates were actually about interpretations, and the Truth was Jesus—a person, not an argument.

These days I still think that, but so many years of pastoral ministry has taught me to see that the Truth tends to wander around beneath all sides of the debates.

The Gospels make it clear that Jesus just kept showing up at the wrong places in society's partisan divides. The Pharisees were angry that he ate with sinners, and the sinners were disappointed that he ate with a Pharisee. He had a clandestine night meeting with the righteous Nicodemus and a very public meeting with an adulterer. He tended to like storms at sea, and he went to a Gentile graveyard to care for a man driven out of his mind by a legion of demons. That was a defiled place for good Jews. He was born, as the incarnation of God, in a very wrong place. In the end the crowds defiled him by throwing him into the house of Pilate, a Gentile, so he could be put on the wrongest place of all—a cross. But he was always still the Truth in all the wrong places. The only place he was unable to do much good was when he went back home to Nazareth, which seems like it should have been the one right place.

We are all writing, speaking, living as partisans of the conflicts that are tearing at the frayed fabric of our society. That may not actually be a problem as long as we all confess that none of us has a leash on the Truth. But that's the problem. We think we're arguing about the truth when we're really just debating interpretations of it.

This even includes interpretations of the Holy Scriptures. In all of the denominational debates I've sat through about gay ordination or marriage, divestment of stocks, or the inequitable distribution of wealth, I've never heard anyone go to the microphone to say, "I would like to represent the lunatic fringe of the church that doesn't give a rip about the Bible." No, they all speak as partisans who have different hermeneutics of the same Bible they all adore.

And we all claim to have spent our lives trying to follow Jesus Christ, the Truth. But like his first disciples, we don't know what to make of the possibility that he may show up on what we think is the wrong side of the debates.

This doesn't mean all sides of debates are valid or even based on the realities of text and history. But it does mean that the Truth can sneak up on you from the other side of the fence. I remember deciding in graduate school that process theology was complete garbage because it claimed God is in the process of "becoming" like the rest of us. There goes the immutable still point of the turning world. I continue to think this theology is mostly very wrong, but one day after reading another journal article advocating it, and preparing to throw it aside, a still small voice whispered to me: "Do you really want a God who can't be affected by what's going on down here?"

I Was Done with Words

I have long forgotten how many baptisms I've performed. But I will never forget this one.

She was three years old, had milk chocolate skin, jet-black hair, and brown eyes the size of saucers. She didn't speak more than a few words of English. We call her Dhini, although her actual name is Vinodhini. Her new father, who is our mission pastor, and his wife had just brought her home from India after spending well over a year struggling to arrange her adoption.

Dhini has some issues. She was born with a large mole on her shoulder that could become cancerous if it's not removed. That involves a series of complicated surgeries and skin grafts that will take years to complete. Also, since she spent her first three years of life in an orphanage where she was left alone most of the day, her motor skills were not so good. And who knows what primal abandonment issues such a little girl may feel?

But there is also the issue of having two parents who are already head over heels in love with her. And the issue of her new congregation that had been praying for her a year before we knew her name. And most of all there is the amazing issue of God's devotion to this precious little girl.

I got through most of the baptismal liturgy pretty well. But when I saw her in the arms of her father, arms around his neck, and I came to the words about being adopted into the family of God, well, you know . . . I was done with words. No one offered to take over for me. The congregation just worshiped a while with tears as our silent prayers of gratitude to God. Eventually, her new father poured the water of a holy covenant over the head of his new daughter. We were all a mess.

Why were we all so overwhelmed by this baptism? Was it that our mission pastor had spent years teaching us how to take the pathos of the world into our hearts? Was it that I had spent even more years preaching about adoption into the Triune family? Maybe. Or perhaps we knew we all have issues, but we pray none of them are greater than the issue of holy love that flows over everything else.

Several years ago the mission pastor and his wife gave birth to a beautiful little blond girl who is now about the same age as Dhini. But through adoption Dhini was made the heir of her parents, and the joint heir of her sister. No one in the congregation missed the metaphor. And that is why we went to pieces when we saw her father ever so gently scoop the water out of the baptismal font and allow it to flow down the face of his new daughter. I noticed that it even dripped onto her wounded shoulder.

Dhini didn't ask to be adopted. She didn't earn or deserve it. She probably didn't know enough even to want it. It just came as a grace that changed everything about her life. That's the way grace works—it is free, unmerited, and unexpected, but then it expects a lot from us. We don't make changes in our life to get adopted; we make them because we have been adopted.

After her adoption this little girl was destined for a lot of work. She has to learn our language, traditions, mission, and she has to understand what it means to wear our family name of Christian. She also has to suffer through the hard work of healing until the marks on her young life can be healed. And she has to figure out what it means to be an Indian raised by Anglo parents. Again, there are so many issues.

Every time we baptize a baby we are launching that child on this same journey through the issues of faith and life. In the sacrament we receive the grace of God, and then we spend the rest of our lives learning how to respond to it. Blessedly this is why we have the church that gives us the language of faith, teaches us its great traditions, inspires us with holy missions for our lives, and constantly points us back to the gospel for our healing. We even have the opportunity to learn how to live with two identities that belong to two kingdoms, this world and the world to come, both of which are created and cherished by God.

Dhini's baptism was two years ago. She's had more surgeries on her shoulder than I can keep count of. But she has never been daunted by any of them and assumes that getting healed is part of her life. Her language skills are now perfect for her age, and her motor skills are wonderful. She's one of the stars of our church's preschool. It's amazing what love can do.

My office at the church looks out over the grassy courtyard that leads to the front door of the preschool. Every time one of Dhini's parents picks up her sister and her after school, they let the girls run with the other children across the grass. Often when I am having a tough day I will look out my office window when I hear the children squealing with delight and laughter as they chase each other.

For some reason Dhini always runs with her hands held straight over her head. Maybe that reason is praise. And maybe that's the real issue that all the adopted children in the family of God need to keep working on.

The Redemption of Early Mistakes

Today we dedicated our new Christian education wing, which was a great joy because we have long needed this facility and because the congregation was so generous that the campaign to raise the funds for the construction was oversubscribed. This was a grace. The last time we tried this, many years ago, it was a huge disaster that was largely my fault.

When I showed up as the new pastor, I was an inexperienced thirty-nine-year-old. The beloved interim pastor Dr. Chesterton, who was at the church two years, was seventy-five. He had recently left a long-term pastorate at a prestigious church in New York and only spent the weekends at our church offering profound, silver-tongued sermons for a couple of years. He told me it was the most enjoyable job he had during his ministry. To use his own words: "It was like a marriage where I never had to do the dishes." He had spent plenty of time doing the dishes in the congregation where he had been installed for over twenty years, and this interim pastoral arrangement was something of a retirement gift. Everyone loved him, including me.

After Dr. Chesterton gave the benediction for the final tear-filled worship service he would serve at our church, a bagpiper came out of nowhere to escort him out the center aisle onto the front lawn where a helicopter was waiting to take him away. When I heard about this all I could think was, "He ascended out of their sight, and they saw him no more." As young as I was, I knew enough to realize none of that adoration automatically transferred to the new pastor.

In those days I was sure that if I worked hard enough I could make anybody love me. Really. I actually thought that. The tragic irony is that all of my frantically spent hours of work only distanced me from everyone who may have been interested in caring about the new pastor. I now wish old Dr. Chesterton would have descended from his helicopter that seemed always to hover overhead, and strolled into my office to say, "You've got to settle down, son. Get to know these folks, and let them take their time to find their way into your heart."

At the end of my first week in the pastor's office I was invited to a "confidential meeting of the church trustees." That sounded intriguing, ominous even, and I of course made sure I was there.

When I entered the room at exactly the time I was told it would begin, I discovered everyone had been at the meeting for a while. They cordially invited me to have a seat. Before I knew it, an architect was at an easel with a pointer describing a new wing of rooms for Christian education classes and church offices. When he was done the trustees all looked at me and asked, "What do you think?"

I remember telling them that it looked like they were talking about a capital campaign and asking if it was a good idea to keep such a notion a secret from the congregation. The chair of the board said, "If we let the congregation know about this, they're going to want to change all of the plans. We think that if you as our new pastor agree this is what we should do, you can make it work. The church will give generously if you're the one asking for its support."

These trustees were a group of very powerful middle-aged leaders of the church who had inherited the board from the older generation that was now too old to go to meetings. All of the trustees were stunning successes in the world of business, but the Old Guard wasn't so sure of their strategies for handling the church's finances. Yet there the new team sat, smiling at me, assuring me that it would just take my endorsement and the money would roll in for this critically needed new wing to the church building.

If such a trap were laid for me today, I would ask the trustees if they were out of their minds to expect a new and unproven pastor to ask the congregation for such sacrificial giving. Who wants to sacrifice spending money for a family vacation to give the church staff better offices? It's ludicrous. But at the time I was blinded by my need to be another adored pastor of the congregation, especially the women and men wearing the power suits. Some of them had kids in our Sunday school who would love to have new classrooms. And the project included new offices, which would make my new staff so pleased with me. So I said, "Sure. We can make this work."

My first phone call was to Brad Davis, the chair of the search committee that brought me to the congregation. I knew he was even more anxious than me about my success in the church and would do anything to help me. Brad was thrilled to be on the inside of this secret plan and quickly agreed to be the chair of the capital campaign that would have to raise millions of dollars to build the new wing. He and I quickly assembled a team of volunteers to give leadership to this new project, half of whom were also on my search committee. None of the trustees was able to help.

We all worked hard on this project after it was presented to the congregation. After a year it was clear to me that while we could raise all the money we needed, we were dividing the congregation over it.

My first clue that we were in trouble came at the congregational meeting to vote on the capital campaign. Our grand idea was to ask Mrs. Moreledge, the surviving widow of one of the previous pastors, to be the honorary chair. Her husband had built the building with a philosophy of ministry that was now way out of date. He was followed by a man who knocked himself out for a dozen years to bring some new life into the congregation. But he finally wandered away broken and exhausted by the loyalists of Pastor Moreledge's ministry, who resisted every innovation. They actually called themselves the Old Guard. Their epicenter was our aging team of male church ushers, who wore morning suits, and even had letterhead that described themselves as "The Usher Corps."

In her capacity as honorary chair of the campaign, dear Mrs. Moreledge had no responsibilities other than to bring along the Old Guard. Since one of my first acts as the new pastor was to officiate at her husband's funeral, she was grateful and happy to serve in this new honorary role. But at the congregational meeting her husband's retired personal attorney went to the microphone, decked out in his Usher Corps suit, to speak against the campaign. "We dare not mortgage our grandchildren's future on such an ill-advised program." He had clearly not been looped into the secret meetings.

Since Mrs. Moreledge was sometimes a bit confused, we asked an elegant young woman to sit next to her on the chancel of the church and help her with the complexities of the meeting.

After the old attorney finished his William Jennings Bryan wannabe speech before the congregation, it became apparent to the young woman that Mrs. Moreledge had been impressed. She knew we were in a bit of trouble. When the time came for a standing vote, the young woman whispered in her ear, "We're not supposed to vote because we're on the leadership team." She didn't realize Mrs. Moreledge was completely deaf in that ear. So after I asked those to stand who were opposed to the motion of proceeding with the capital campaign, the honorary chair rose from her very public seat in the chancel to stand proudly, clutching her patent leather purse with both hands.

During the long months that followed that disastrous congregational meeting, I could never get that capital campaign out of the ditch. The younger half of the congregation rallied and mailed in their pledges, but I never got the feeling that they believed in what we were trying to build. I now think they just didn't want the stogy Old Guard Moreledge people to prevent another creative idea from going forward like they did during my predecessor's entire tenure. And the trustees were as gone as little boys who start a fire in a field and run for hiding to watch it burn.

After a year, it finally occurred to me that I had been snookered. I would love to say that realization came to me in a moment of revelation, but it actually took a lot of 4:00 a.m., wide-awake staring at the ceiling ponderings to realize this. I wasn't leading the church. I was being its pawn in a very old family chess game designed to ensure no one could win. I was really tired of it, and my only hope was that the members of the congregation were also fed up with their roles of being worried about each other.

At the benediction following worship one Sunday, I surprised everyone by saying something like,

> We've been at this capital campaign for almost a year. But it has mostly worn us out and heightened our divisions. I didn't come here to divide the church, and I don't want to build church buildings only to hurt the body of Christ. So please hear my apology for using your pulpit to proclaim this was God's will before I got to know our church family well. We're not old versus young, or past versus future. We're just a strange family that Christ created. I think we should set aside this capital campaign until we've had the time to develop a common vision of our future.

In all of my years of pastoral ministry, that was the only time I've ever received a standing ovation. And it came as a response to an apology.

That was a long time ago, and it's now no surprise to me that we decided the building campaign could wait its turn behind more pressing agendas, like the local urban mission programs we developed with James Kairns's church. But we eventually had to do something about the building whose problems were piling up. With more than a little trepidation I agreed to take a second stab at a campaign, which cost over twice as much as the original.

This time the money rolled in. It was about the easiest project I've seen our church take on. But it's significant that the failed first attempt cost a lot of time before we could try again. That wasn't a punishment from the congregation. It was just fear of not wanting to mess up a thriving ministry with an old family argument.

Most of the Old Guard is dead now, and the ushers' morning suits went away long ago when we insisted they start recruiting women. But about a third of the money we raised for this new building program came from their bequests designated "for the next capital campaign." It's striking that we've received so many bequests with that same specific focus. Clearly, the old folks were writing to each other and came up with their own secret plan to help us.

I'm sure they used the Usher Corps letterhead.

The Loss of Saturday Nights

Last Sunday we had a guest preacher, one of the missionaries our church supports. That meant I was free on Saturday night, which is a novelty to Ellie and me.

On Saturday evenings, our house always goes into monastery mode. If the sermon is not done, I am in The Study frantically trying to pull a line or two down from heaven that will make holy sense of the message I've been working on all week. Even if it is done, I'll still spend Saturday night poring over it, changing it, but not really improving it. Long ago I realized this is just a way of getting ready to enter the pulpit with the audacity to say, "Hear the Word of the Lord."

When Mackenzie was a teenager, she never invited her friends over to the house for sleepovers on Saturday night. The house was too depressingly quiet. And when Ellie brought in the mail that contained an invitation to a Saturday night party, she sighed with disappointment knowing that if she really wanted to go she'd have to show up alone and make a lot of excuses for my absence.

Saturday night is when I enter the Holy of Holies and place on the altar everything I have been working on all week. If I think it's an acceptable sacrifice, I know I have to give it back to the Holy, who may have as little regard for it as for Cain's offering. And if I think it is an unworthy offering, which is typical, then I just have to humbly say, "This is all I have, God. If you have better ideas, I'm all ears."

I always try to spend the first three hours of the morning every day of the week in The Study with the holy words of the biblical text and the ordinary words I have collected from my parishioners, trying to maintain the sacred conversation between them. The Study is the crucible where these words get mixed together and provide the next sermon.

Sometimes the congregation and God speak to each other so rapidly that they're talking past each other. I can barely keep up. At other times they're giving each other the silent treatment. That's when Saturday night becomes dramatic. Over the years I've learned that any argument between the congregation and God is a lover's quarrel, and neither of them can avoid each other for long. It's always a holy word that breaks the silence through the biblical text, and by Sunday morning there is always something to say from the Lord. But no matter how hard I've worked on the sermon, and even if the line from heaven came earlier in the week, Saturday night is still the time when my sermon is transformed from a document I'll recite from the pulpit into the Word of the Lord. I never talk to God more honestly, fluently, and passionately than on Saturday nights.

But when there's a Saturday that I'm not expected to be in the pulpit the following day, I get to return to civilian life.

Every time I take my summer vacation, and there are several free weekends piled together, I tell Ellie the same thing: "I get why people don't come to worship." An evening spent at an elegant dinner on Saturday, followed by a leisurely Sunday morning with a cup of Starbucks and the *New York Times*, sounds pretty good to me too. So when I climb into the pulpit and look at the congregation, I have two emotional responses to seeing them in the pews.

The first is envy. Unlike me, they came to worship this morning because they were free. They could have set up a tennis game. But they chose to come to worship because they knew it to be good for their souls. By contrast, I was in church that morning because it was my job to have a word from the Lord for them.

The second emotion is admiration. There are so many other compelling invitations for how the congregation could have used their morning, and they gain no social capital for being in church, but they chose to listen to their soul's insatiable thirst for another word of holiness.

Ellie and I used our free Saturday night to catch a movie and a pizza afterward. We enjoyed the entertainment, and certainly the time together, but our souls felt nothing.

Call Finds a Way

Alexander Edison came to see me again today. I was wondering how his application to Harvard had gone, but was not surprised when he began by dropping his head and shoulders again as he said, "Well, I didn't get into Harvard."

I asked him what he was feeling about that.

He didn't say anything for a while but finally said, "My parents are pretty upset."

Knowing it was doubtful that I would get far with this, I tried again by asking, "How do you feel about not going to Harvard?"

He surprised me by sitting tall in the chair and saying, "I don't know what any of us were thinking. Me going to Harvard? That's ludicrous. Mostly I am just feeling embarrassed that I applied."

I started to ask him why he applied, but he knew that I knew why he applied, and he cut me off.

Almost tearfully he jumped on me with, "You think this was all just my parents' dream, but I would have loved to show them I got into the toughest school in the country."

"I'm sure you would have loved that."

Another pause.

"But I never thought about actually being there. My guess is that I wouldn't have enjoyed it so much, and I doubt I'd have survived there for long."

Then I tentatively asked, "So why are you here today, Alexander?" He was ready for that. "I want you to respect my parents. They've sacrificed so much for me and my little sister because they love us and only want what is best."

"I believe that's true," I said. "What do you think is best?" He looked at me like I was crazy and said, "Well, Harvard is best. But that's not happening. I've been accepted to a couple of the safety schools where I applied. So I can still go to college."

Then he bit his lip for a while and said, "I've grown up in this church, so you're the only pastor I know. I want to know if you think we all have a purpose to our lives."

Perhaps too quickly I said, "Yes, of course I think that. You've heard me say it more than once. But I also think it takes a long time to discover that purpose. And usually you don't know it until you've been fulfilling it for a while. But I'm confident God's purpose in creating you was for something far greater than getting into Harvard. For that matter it's far greater than whatever job you take after finishing college."

"Yeah, that sounds like you," he said smiling at me.

"Okay. So what are you going to do now?" I asked.

"Well, one of the schools where I got accepted is Southwest Minnesota State University. It has a program in culinary arts. I've always loved to cook, and I already make half the family dinners because my parents always get home so late from work. I don't know if I can succeed at that either, but I do know I would love to try."

I couldn't help myself. "What do your parents think of that idea?"

Then it came. "Well, see, they know about me having to go to one of the safety schools, but not about the culinary program. I was wondering if you could talk to them."

To myself I thought, *Yeah, that sounds like you.* But to Alexander I said, "Nah, thanks for the invitation but this is a conversation you're going to need to have with them on your own."

"They're going to blow."

"Maybe. Maybe not. But this is your life, and it's time to start claiming it. Again, that's part of God's purpose for you."

Alexander's agenda for the meeting was over, so he was getting his coat on to leave.

I asked one more question. "Why did you apply to this particular school? It's nowhere near here."

"Like I said, I needed a safety school and was pretty sure I could get into it."

Almost winking at him I said, "So you chose a safety school halfway across the country that just happened to have a culinary program?"

"Yeah, my folks are probably going to figure that out also."

"Yes," I said, "I'd be surprised if they haven't already. Give them the chance to get on board with this idea. And the one after that if it doesn't work out. They love you, remember?"

He nodded, "Yeah, they do. But they're really disappointed."

I know Alexander's parents well, but I have no idea if they can make the very sharp turn from Harvard to Southwest Minnesota State's culinary program. I do know that it's my job to keep presenting hope and another chance to families. And I know that parents who really love their children eventually sacrifice their dreams for them.

April

Week One

Struggling to Say "Behold"

My devotional this morning returned me to the twenty-seventh psalm, where King David reveals his soul's greatest yearning.

> One thing have I asked of the Lord, that will I seek after: to live in the house of the Lord all the days of my life, to behold the beauty of the Lord, and to inquire in his temple.

I've been thinking about this all day. It's so compelling to hear people say they know the one thing they're seeking. I wonder when it was exactly that David decided he was just interested in worship because it allowed him to behold beauty and seek truth.

I wonder if my parishioners get this when they take their places in the dark oak pews on Sunday morning, fretting about all they have to get done before the business meeting on Monday, or the pile of laundry they left in the bedroom before coming to church. There are so many times when I'm leading worship that even I miss its true goal. It's easy for me to get focused on the microphone that's still not working, or why the associate pastor decided to turn the pastoral prayer into a homily, or the homeless person wandering down the center aisle in the middle of the sermon, that I miss the point of why we all gathered in a holy sanctuary. We were dragged there by our souls that didn't bother explaining why.

Pastors are far from angels, but our job calls us to use the angels' favorite word, "Behold," quite a bit. We're supposed to get people to stop being so distracted by their anxieties, fleeting pleasures, deep regrets, loneliness, and frantic efforts to save themselves through more hard work in order to spend one hour beholding the holy landscape on which they live.

Every time I put a worship service together I'm trying to present the twins of beauty and truth to the congregation. The call to worship, the absolution after the confession, the homily, the creed, and certainly the sacraments are all a way of beholding God's beauty and petitioning for some beautiful word of truth to pierce through the distorted world in which we live.

Occasionally someone will come through the line at the door following worship, shake my hand, and say, "Well, that was nice. Now it's back to reality." It takes everything careful in me to resist taking that person by the neck and yelling, "Don't you get it? You just had an hour of the most real thing you will encounter this week. You stood before Holy, Holy, Holy. Now it is time to return to your mission to witness the beauty and truth of this holiness in a society that is so distracted it has no idea how to see it. This worship service was designed to wipe the smudges off your spectacles so you could behold. The people around you need to believe that at least you believe."

I don't say any of that. I just chuckle and respond with a "yes" so I can keep the line moving. But a voice inside my own soul says, *Swing and a miss. They still don't get it.*

That's why I am here. If they understood the holy claims on their lives, they wouldn't need a pastor. Next Sunday I will have another at-bat.

As a Protestant congregation, we have a harder time beholding beauty than we do inquiring in God's temple, as if the sixteenth-century Reformation rupture caused a divorce in the church, and in the settlement the Catholics took custody of beholding beauty while we got inquiring in the temple. That's what Protestants are known for—lots of words. We study them, memorize them, preach and teach them, write more words about words, and often use them to beat each other on the head with judgment. But beauty scares us.

When Luther and Calvin were using so many words to explain their desired reformation of the church they already knew all about the beatific visions of Bernard of Clairvaux, Teresa of Ávila, and Julian of Norwich. What is striking to me is that they never tried to debunk any of the visions. They just thought they were unnecessary, and the same vision of God's beauty could be found through an encounter with the words in the Bible.

That's my tradition. I don't have any sculptures of saints having ecstatic visions or Renaissance paintings hanging around the halls of the church. All I have are words. We say them in the creed, sing them in hymns, hear the biblical text being read, and listen as still more words are proclaimed from the pulpit.

But by the time people come to worship on Sunday morning, they have already been buffeted by so many words that have been used to manipulate, hurt, spin facts, and peddle things they don't really need. Someone made promises to them, but it turned out to be just words. When the pastor stands in the pulpit and says, "Hear the Word of the Lord," they aren't expecting to encounter either beauty or truth. Mostly, they're just hoping I'll be entertaining and brief. It's my job to smuggle in something that can change their lives.

Words are as powerful as the fusion of atoms. No one ever forgets hearing the first time a sweet young person said, "I love you." Nor does anyone ever forget hearing, "You're not the smart one" or "That's not good enough." For good or bad, words lead us either to the beauty of God's love or back to the desperate struggle of navigating life without grace.

This is why it's hard for me to get to bed on Saturday night. Even if the sermon is long done and put to bed, I stay up poring over it as it sleeps. I need to ensure that these are not just more words banging around the pews. The sermon has to help people behold.

Nothing I do is harder, or more rewarding, than this part of my calling. And it just keeps coming every Sunday.

Week Two

The Real Problem
with Being Visible

This morning I met with a group of young students from the seminary who told me they had a class assignment to interview a working pastor. It was affirming to assume that I was a "working" pastor. There are days when I wonder about that.

They asked several very good questions, but the one to which they kept returning was about visibility. They're really worried about that. I think they wanted me to tell them they didn't need to worry about being pastors on display for everyone to see and then talk about.

To their dismay, I told them that of course as pastors they would be incredibly visible.

Everyone in our congregation knows pretty much everything about my house because most of them have been in it. They know about my daughter, how bad my golf game is, what my wife wore at the grocery store last week, that I appear to be putting on weight, and what kind of car I drive. If I get a new car, the news travels quickly. I tried to reassure the seminarians that this is the easy part. Either you get used to this in the first few years of your ministry or you get out.

The harder thing, which they haven't considered, is the spiritual visibility. The church has ordained me to maintain a sacred conversation between them and the God who is their only comfort in life and death. That assumes God and I are on speaking terms. And there's nothing more spiritually vulnerable than preaching, when it's done well. So for the congregation's sake, I have to keep my soul healthy.

Flight attendants tell us to place the oxygen masks on ourselves before fitting them on others. Couples learn the secret to intimacy is being self-sufficient so there is someone for the other person to keep loving. And pastors eventually learn there is nothing more important they can do for their congregations than maintain their spiritual disciplines.

There may be unhealthy congregations with a visionary healthy pastor, but there is no such thing as a healthy congregation with an unhealthy pastor. When pastors go down, they take the whole church with them. This is the subtext of what my parishioners really mean when they shake my hand and say, "I'm praying for you."

Old Brad Davis, the chair of the search committee that brought me to the church so long ago, has an annoying habit of asking me how my devotional life is going. I hate it when he does that. But I really need it. And he needs me to need it.

Week Three

Hard Lessons on Flannelgraph

Whenever I can, I try to walk around the children's Sunday school classes between worship services. There are also adult classes going on, but I've learned that if I even stick my head in the door, the teacher and participants will become anxious that I'm checking up on things. The kids never think that and are always happy to have me join their circle.

This morning, I found some of our kids sitting around a TV monitor that was presenting the latest VeggieTales cartoon depicting another biblical story. I love this series, smiled when I saw them so entranced, and took the nodding teacher's invitation to take a seat and join them. The children don't assume the guy in a clerical collar is anything more than that, and they are happy to have me plop down on one of their amazingly small chairs.

As I watched the video I remembered that when I was in third grade, the state-of-the-art teaching device was flannelgraph. It was a large board wrapped in, well, flannel perched on an easel. The teacher, always Mrs. Williams, would place the biblical characters on the board as she told the biblical story about their life. For some reason there was always a camel lying down under a palm tree already on the flannelgraph before she began the story. I can still see Mrs.

Williams's long bony fingers moving back and forth over the paper characters who arrived for her telling of the story, trying to smooth them out and get them to stick into their place on the drama.

Whenever the apostle Paul was used in one of her stories, he took a lot of extra smoothing out beneath her fingers. That's because he had been overused in the stories. One of our greatest delights as kids was getting to hand Mrs. Williams the next character to be placed on her flannelgraph. One day Johnny Burke and I fought over who would have this high honor, and our tugging against each other tore the little apostle's head off. So he was taped together. And some other kids—I'm thinking it was those outsiders in Vacation Bible School—spilled purple Kool-Aid all over him. But Mrs. Williams couldn't stop using the apostle in her stories. He just came up too often in her biblical dramas.

Mrs. Williams was proclaiming to the children in her classes a holy mystery she never intended to communicate—God is not easy on the people used in the holy drama. By the end of their lives, even the best of them were taped together and discolored. The apostle Paul had been chased out of half the cities in the Roman Empire by the end of his life, typically with a shower of rocks behind him. But when he wrote one of his last letters to the Philippians from jail, all he wanted to talk about was his surpassing joy. I think that's because his life's delight was that he got used in the biblical drama. As Abraham, Moses, Rahab, and David's lives also depict, a leader's only fear is that failure might cast them aside from the drama of God's redemptive work with mere mortals.

This is part of what it means to be called to be a pastor. The calling doesn't come our way because we deserve it. We don't. It comes only because God chooses to use flawed creatures to take a role in the high drama of proclaiming grace to all who are taped together and stained by life. God doesn't protect pastors. How could that be if the message to all is, "I know what you've done, left undone, and what's been done to you. But I'm dying to love you."

Week Four

Finally Loving Easter

The Easter worship service this morning was, as usual, anything but subtle. Like everyone else in the crowded sanctuary, I love all the fuss of this day—the brass instruments blaring out "Jesus Christ Is Risen Today" as if to dare the congregation to match their volume, the ubiquitous lilies, the little girls reminding me of Mackenzie's love for her new Easter dresses, and best of all the jam-packed pews. For much of my ministry I found the annual return of Easter to be a source of great stress, mostly because of the sermon. I used to hammer myself with the need to make this sermon "really count." If you asked me why, I would have said it's because this is the day when we proclaim the resurrection, which is at the core of our faith. But if you wandered into my stress-filled heart you would have discovered that the real problem was the jam-packed pews.

Maybe in those days I was thinking that if the sermon was really good, all those guests would come back next week. Maybe I was under some messianic illusion that if I presented the resurrection in a way that was moving, convincing, or at least not boring, those who were on the margins of faith would say, "Okay, now I believe." Or maybe I just saw Easter as the big show, and I didn't want to blow it in front of all those people.

None of those old hopes for the sermon on the resurrection ever came true. The Sunday after Easter was always one of the lowest attended of the year. No one ever stopped at the door of the sanctuary after my Easter sermon to make a new confession of faith. And I'm sure that everyone in those packed pews already knew essentially what I was going to be preaching about before I ever stepped into the pulpit. They were thinking, "He's going to say something about Christ being risen from the dead. And he'll tell us that's good news." That's always exactly what I did, but never adequately. For years I drove home from Easter Sunday wondering if I was too old to apply to law school.

Driving home from church today, I started wondering when I moved from being stressed by Easter to really loving it. It certainly wasn't because I figured out how to handle that sermon. The message isn't just good news; it's so world-changing no preacher could ever do it justice. The best preachers approach Easter like the women who saw the empty tomb and then tore out of the cemetery with their robes hiked up to their knees. They had to tell somebody, even though no one took their word for it.

My hunch is that like most things I have come to love and enjoy, the path to finding the blessing of Easter was a forced humility. Maybe even surrender. I can't control the message that Christ is risen. It controls me. I can't even get to the bottom of its meaning, let alone figure out how to attractively package it for a twenty-minute sermon. But I know that, somehow, the resurrection of Christ is at the bottom of me. Of all of us. It's our only hope. And the older I get the more I believe that the old apostle knew in his bones what he was writing about when he claimed that if Christ isn't raised from the dead, everything else falls apart.

I have buried too many good people who died too soon, sat beside too many people after they heard their disease is incurable, counseled too many couples whose marriage was clearly falling apart, and felt too discouraged with the promises of the church, my favorite politicians, and most of all my own aspira-tions. There is ultimately no hope in medicine, therapy, activism, or even the church's mission. And I certainly have no reason to hope in a preacher who can't even pull together a convincing Eas-ter sermon.

But beneath all of this disappointment is the Savior. The reason he's a savior is that he won't settle for just being with us in the mess we've made. That's why the gospel is good news. Jesus is always calling us to come out of our tombs.

I have long been struck by the way the Gospel according to St. John depicts the raising of Lazarus from the dead. I've been to the place that tradition calls the tomb of Lazarus in Bethany. It's a cold, dark cave, burrowed deep down into the earth. The reality is that everyone has visited their own version of that tomb, and often. It's where we go when we lose interest in life because the disappointments are just too great.

After telling the people at the tomb to remove the stone, Jesus stands at the open door and calls for Lazarus to "come forth." It seems significant to me that Jesus doesn't go into the tomb to comfort the dead man. He doesn't say, "You were a victim. You got robbed because I didn't get to you in the nick of time to prevent you from dying. But at least you're not alone because I am down here now with you to offer a little comfort."

That's what we would like. We want Jesus to help us make sense of our losses, or at least put us at ease in our tombs. But Jesus doesn't like tombs. He didn't spend much time in his own tomb, and he's not coming into ours. Instead, he stands at the door and says, "Why are you settling for this despair? The grief was supposed to be a long, hard journey, but not your soul friend. It's time to come back to life. The door's open. All you have to do is come forth."

I'll never understand why Jesus so often prefers to show up *after* the nick of time has come and gone, after we've been let down by everything else we asked him to use to save us. But I do know his nature is to bring light into the darkness of despair. This is at the core of the hope I keep trying to preach.

What is important is not how inadequately I present the hope, but that for thousands of years this hope is the most real thing the church has believed. In the resurrection of Christ, death is no longer the final chapter of any story. There is always the invitation to come out of the tomb.

Somewhere along the line I got less interested in my ability to talk about this stunning hope, and so much more devoted to believing it. I'm thinking that's when I began to enjoy Easter. Maybe that's why I also enjoyed seeing the jam-packed pews today. Maybe it wasn't their mothers but their souls that dragged them to church today to hear the words, "Come forth."

May

The Beloved Horse's Ass

I keep thinking about the sixtieth wedding anniversary celebration I attended last week. It was put together by the kids of Gene and Gladys Riley to honor their parents' long years of faithful commitment. The evening was filled with laughter, stories, and a new song written and sung by their granddaughter while her sister played guitar so tentatively. Gladys is about as gracious a person as I have ever met, but Gene has always been a strangely attractive curmudgeon. Last fall when I helped Gladys convince him it was time to give up driving, he put up quite an argument but then seemed almost grateful that we were helping him with a decision he couldn't make on his own. He's always been like that.

Several months after I began my ministry at the church I met Gene at a worship committee meeting. We were supposed to be talking about a motion that had been presented by the Usher Corps that would allow them to hold late visitors at the doors of the sanctuary until the prayer of confession was over. But Gene hijacked the meeting when he started complaining about a decision the trustees had made to repaint the sanctuary. That would mean a summer of worshiping with scaffolding in our way.

I gently indicated that I had been there when the trustees made their decision and said, "It was a tough call, and no one likes scaffolding in a sanctuary, but I think the trustees made the best choice possible. And it's not like this is happening over Advent or Easter." Gene leaned across the table as he said, "There are such easier and cheaper ways to paint the sanctuary. And if you think the trustees are right to sign this ridiculous contract, you're a horse's ass."

I'm not sure which offended me more: that this man had just publicly called his new pastor a horse's ass or that no one else in the committee meeting seemed particularly bothered by it. There was an awkward pause, and then we went on with the agenda.

When the meeting was over, Gene stuck around. It was clear he wanted to speak with me as soon as I was done talking with the committee chair about how we would follow up on the decisions the committee had made. After Gene and I were alone in the room, I assumed he had stayed behind to apologize for his inappropriate comment. Instead he said, "I just wanted you to know that I am so grateful God brought you to our church. Every night Gladys and I end our day by getting on our knees by our bed in prayer. And we always pray for you." Then he embraced me, turned, and left the room.

It took me a while to realize that both things Gene said that night were completely authentic to what he thought about his pastor. He really did believe God had called me to serve his church, and he prayed for me at the end of every hard day. And he really did think I was an ass for doing something he believed to be wrong.

Over the long years that have followed that strange committee meeting, there have been quite a few conversations with Gene that ended in something similar to him calling me an ass, and many more when he had tender words of encouragement, and several when he again said both in the same meeting. It took me quite a while to figure out that Gene wasn't a bit bothered that I thought he could also be an ass, but he would have been horrified if anyone suggested I wasn't called to be the pastor of his church.

My country grandmother hated her pastor for thirty years. But it never occurred to her to leave the church, nor did her pastor have any intention of looking for a new congregation where everyone would be unconditionally in awe of him. When I was a seminarian visiting Grandma, she again wandered into her misgivings about her pastor. But she would always conclude her latest complaint by saying, "Bless his heart," and it wasn't sarcastic. I reminded her that I had often heard this lament from her over the years and wondered why she didn't just leave the church. Grandma paused while looking me dead in the eye and said, "Thou shalt not lift up thy hand against the Lord's anointed." I was pretty sure that was not one of the Ten Commandments, but it certainly was for her.

I think Gene and my grandma went to the same school. They learned a higher view of calling than most congregations have today. The pastor, they thought, is the pastor and you can't get rid of the pastor just because she or he can be an ass at times. These days I watch so many pastors get tossed by their congregations for the slightest infractions.

To be "the Lord's anointed" is not a Get Out of Jail Free card. It just means that everyone, including God, believes that the pastor and the congregation have been thrown together. The relationship may or may not work out in the end, and along the way there will certainly be lots of stepping on each other's toes. But it's critical that everyone give up the idea that the pastor should be adored. It's especially important that the pastor abandon this illusion.

Most weeks the congregation doesn't even adore God, but they still come back into the sanctuary every Sunday because their souls have called them to worship. And the pastor is called to help them worship well. No one has to like it all the time. We don't even have to like each other, which is really beside the point.

But life falls apart if we wander away from our calling to worship together.

Week Two

Getting It Wrong with Race and Gender

I received a brochure today inviting me to attend a local pastors' conference led by the Reverend Angela Thomas. Many years ago Angela was our new associate pastor for missions at St. Andrews. I had recruited her after she finished seminary as one of my students because I knew she was incredibly gifted and destined to be a leader in the community, and I thought it was high time we had an African American pastor on our staff.

She agreed to come, with some trepidation since we are mostly a white congregation. But she trusted me and my vision for partnerships with minority faith communities. So when the job was offered, she took it.

Even though our church thinks of itself as socially sophisticated, I knew that I needed to prepare them to receive their first Black pastor on the team. I tried to pierce through their need to agree to the politically correct response to my proposal, and wanted to ensure they knew they were asking for leadership from someone who had a different story from us. "She will lead us to places we may be hesitant to go," I kept saying. All the conversations went well, and I was constantly reassured the church was not only willing but also eager. The congregational vote to hire her was unanimous. It wasn't even unanimous when they voted on my election to be the senior pastor. I thought we were all set.

At the evening service when Angela was ordained and installed as one of our pastors, I had the privilege of placing the ministerial stole around her neck and publicly saying, "You are now one of our pastors." It was a great moment of hope for the church and for Angela, although I had a hunch that she still had her doubts.

The following two years of her ministry were fabulous for the congregation but not for Angela. She worked hard for us, but it was clear that she was always holding something back. Or maybe protecting some part of herself.

Her preaching, pastoral care, and revitalization of our mission program were all fantastic. But by the end of her second year with us two problems became clear.

The first was that Angela was growing weary of being the symbol of a church that took pride in having an African American pastor. She missed singing the songs of faith with Black sisters and brothers who shared her story. Our very White liturgy, culture, bureaucracy, and vestments became heavy on her shoulders. We were not an easy yoke for her to bear. We called Angela to be one of our pastors, but without realizing it we were actually asking her to be a missionary to a White church. That's a different calling.

She wanted to be a pastor among a people she understood and who understood her. She could never get over the feeling that she was a stranger in a clerical collar.

The second problem was revealed to me when I was at a church picnic. A fourteen-year-old white girl in the congregation came up to me, with her mother standing behind her. She tenderly said, "Thank you for bringing a woman to be one of our pastors." At that moment it hit me that I had been so focused on the racial issues of having an African American pastor I had totally missed the stark reality that I was also asking the church to hire its first female associate pastor. There were no conversations, preparation, or encouragement about what it would mean to accept leadership from a woman wearing a stole in worship. I had assumed that the church was way beyond that issue. The congregation included women who were judges, doctors, and great models of success in business. At least half of our elders were women. But after the conversation with the teenager at the picnic my ponderings became focused on how revolutionary it was for this sophisticated congregation to see a woman in their pulpit. Had I asked the members of the church if they were comfortable having a woman as one of their pastors, they would have said, "Of course." But I failed to get beneath their "of course" to make sure they realized how a woman would challenge their preconceptions of what a pastor should look like.

Angela was the new pastor who had to take on two mission fields—our Whiteness and our familiarity with male clergy. Neither of those was in her job description.

When a Black church in the area invited her to become their pastor she quickly accepted. She told me that she had done what she could, but it was time to go home. I wanted to assure her that I understood, but the disappointment overwhelmed me.

Churches always make a mistake when they hire a young pastor thinking that will bring more young people into the congregation. We made a mistake in thinking that if we hired a Black pastor she would help us be more diverse. I should have known better. Before St. Andrews tries this again, we need to sort through why we are so white in a community that's so racially diverse. How do we remain true to who we are, who we've always been, while embracing who we can be?

And what do I learn from this about my own calling? It's a clumsy time to be a socially progressive white male pastor. I agree with most of the social critique that claims I had privileges in my career path that women and minorities did not. I keep telling myself I was never interested in a career, and just wanted to be a pastor. But there's an unavoidable corporate nature to the church. Then I try telling myself that I've worked really hard to get to my position in the church. That's true, but I realize that in every interview for a job along the way my white guy card was sitting on the table. I am now ineffectively trying to change a church that let me succeed more easily than those who were not white males.

How can I be both prophet and complicit? As Joe Lincoln would say, it just keeps coming back to life as a humility to the end. If that casts me upon the grace of our common Savior, humility is good news.

The Adored Director of Music

Today I had lunch with Jon Ahlstrom, who retired from being our director of music about five years ago. He was in town to see his daughter and her family, who are still members of the congregation.

Jon was serving the church long before I arrived. He came directly to our congregation as a young graduate of an esteemed choir college. He took over the organ and choir from a giant in the field, who also stayed most of his career at the church. The way Jon tells it, things were rough for him at first because people weren't sure the new kid had it in him to succeed. But in time he convinced most of the congregation he was really good at this job, and he outlived those who refused to be convinced. By the time he retired, he was also a giant in the field with a large portfolio of published hymns and choral anthems.

After Jon left we hired a young woman from the same choir college, and the hand-wringing started again. Not surprisingly, the leader of the rebel band was Jon's daughter. But Mrs. Parker, the former clerk of session, threw her considerable influence behind the new director of music and made a lot of phone calls from her assisted living facility. That helped a lot, but I still suffered through lots of appointments of "concern" over the direction of the music program. All of that settled down several years ago.

Directors of music often elicit strong emotions in a congregation. I suppose that's because the people in the pews have high expectations for the music they receive in worship. I understand that. I have spent my life with words because I believe they're powerful. Put together carefully, the right words can change a life. But thrown together in anger, words can do more harm than can ever be repaired. But music can travel deeper into the heart than words alone can ever go. Even ridiculously thin, politically correct words put to good music can get inside you. (See the new hymnbook.) So there's a lot at stake when a new music director arrives. And when a new pastor arrives, the congregation holds its breath to see how the relationship with the music director works out.

Upon my arrival as the new pastor, it was immediately clear to me that Jon was a force to be reckoned with in the congregation. Some of the pastoral search committee privately cautioned me about this while others openly praised him as one of the "jewels of the congregation." I soon discovered for myself that they were all correct. Jon really was great at his job, he clearly loved the church, and he very much enjoyed the high esteem in which he was held.

The senior pastor who preceded me had a rocky tenure with many in the congregation, and a publicly difficult relationship with Jon. Those difficulties were intertwined. The Jon Ahlstrom loyalists credited his leadership of the worship music program as the single thread that held the church together through those hard days. The Holy Spirit may have also had something to do with keeping the church together, but I didn't bring that up too often.

Early on, I felt threatened by Jon's popularity in the congregation. I kept waiting for our troubles with each other to begin as they had with my predecessor. It never occurred to me that Jon was worried about the same thing, but he later confessed to being very anxious during my first year as the pastor. I wonder if in those days we were two reluctant wrestlers circling each other, ready to lock arms if the other attacked. But it never happened. I think that's because I eventually figured out it didn't cost me a thing for Jon to be adored. And while Jon enjoyed the adoration, he never felt the need to take it for a spin to see how far his influence could go in the church. Mostly he just wanted to make great worship music. He was happy to let me lead the church as long as I didn't run it off a cliff, which wasn't in my plans.

Ironically, I knew that Jon and I were going to be okay when we finally stopped complimenting each other all the time like we did the first year. The subtext of all those "great job today" comments after every worship service was, "I'd rather not be your enemy." After we got that out of our system, we found the ground between us safe enough to be a creative space where we could weave the biblical text, sermon, and music of the worship service into a common tapestry that we rolled out every Sunday. But none of that was going to happen until Jon and I got tired of worrying about each other. We never really became friends, but we worked extremely well together as colleagues who shared a common devotion to giving the adoration to God more than collecting it for ourselves.

Our compliments to each other still came through the long years we worked together, but they were rare enough to have meaning. And they were focused on how we had helped the congregation. Today he complimented me on the choice for his successor. I told him it wouldn't hurt for him to mention that to his daughter.

You're Dead Right

The retirement party is coming up in a month. I tried to talk the planning committee out of having it in an expensive hotel ballroom. I pleaded with them for no band, no program, and no dignitaries from the city or the presbytery. I explained again that I wasn't looking for a celebration of my ministry. Neither was Ellie. At the January meeting of the elders, when the retirement celebration planning committee was formed, I thought I had made this clear. What we wanted was just a comfortable place to say I love you, and that it's time for us to go now.

Our idea was that this event should be another church potluck in the fellowship hall, just like all the ones we've had over all our circling years in this parish. In my plea to the planning committee I waxed poetic and sentimental about how perfect it would be to have one last overly cooked lasagna dinner together, sitting at folding tables covered with the stained red-and-white gingham tablecloths. "And the only gifts should be the pies that people bring for the dinner."

I am not without clout in this church. I've always tried to be a careful steward of that, and most of the time I keep it holstered.

But on the rare occasions that I say, "This is what we should do," the folks around me usually say, "Well, okay then, if you feel that strongly about it."

But not this time. Today I learned we're having the retirement party in the soulless hotel ballroom.

The church elder who is the chair of the planning committee made an appointment to see me because she knows how much I wanted this event to be low-key. Apparently, I've made the point more than once to members of her committee. I was impressed with how well she broke the news to me. She started by reminding me of the many years we've worked together in the church, and then went on to describe specific controversies in the congregation when the elders and their pastors stood together. She said she couldn't even imagine a situation in which the lay leadership of the church would ever publicly disagree with me—until now.

I responded by taking one more try at the beauty of having our kind of church dinner, in our kind of room, to say our kind of goodbye. She sat silently through the familiar little homily. When I was done, all she said was that I was "dead right."

That was dirty pool, because branding a choice as "dead right" is something she's heard from me for years. It means being so correct that you're spiritually dead. Like the Pharisees. Or being so correct it'll kill you. Like insisting on your right to cross an intersection when a garbage truck is screaming through a red light. Or being so correct you're not loving. Like insisting on a potluck dinner for my retirement party when the congregation needs to make a fuss about its pastor. With just two words she won the argument.

As I've let this sink in today, I find myself smiling a lot. I'm still dreading the hotel ballroom and the loss of my dream for this goodbye, but I somehow feel even better about the retirement. One of the ways a pastor knows it's time to leave is when the congregation can give the sermons they've been hearing over the years.

I do love these people far more than my dreams. I thought I had settled that debate within me a long time ago, but here at the end I was being given one more opportunity to let love win.

Dad, Not Pastor

My grandson took a date to his high school prom. Since he had never spoken about her before, his parents assumed it was just a way for both of them to get into the prom. But according to Mackenzie, since the prom he's used every free evening to "hang out" with her.

There is so much language that has changed over the generations, but I find it striking that kids today still use "hanging out" as a euphemism to describe a date. "No big deal. We're just hanging out." What they don't realize is that such seemingly innocuous language is actually betraying a stark reality—their tender young hearts really are hanging out there and thus vulnerable to what may happen. And don't get me started on the phrase "hooking up."

It now appears that my grandson has been smitten by a beautiful young Mormon. I'm a tad concerned by this, but mostly I'm amused by my daughter's inclination to pass out constantly with anxiety. "I will not be the grandmother to little Mormons," she lamented over the phone tonight. I tried to reassure her that her son is just seventeen years old, we have no idea if this new infatuation will go the distance, and they're heading to different colleges. If Mackenzie were my parishioner I would say, "Who knows? If they get married and have babies, you will in fact be the grandmother of little Mormons." But she's not my parishioner.

So I boldly told her, "This will never last."

I eventually learned to resist making such ridiculous prophetic claims when responding to my parishioners' anxieties. Instead I helped them envision the worst-case scenario to their worry, and then pressed the question—so what then? My hope was to help them discover the redemptive presence of God even if their darkest fears came true.

But all of that good pastoral care goes out the window when I talk with my daughter. With her I am just supposed to be her dad, who says reassuring dad-like things. That's all she really wants, and as I've learned the hard way, it's my only place in her life. I can do that now, but it took a long time for me to figure out how.

After the phone call, I stared at the wall thinking about all of the time I've wasted trying to be an exemplary pastor in front of her. And my hunch is so did she.

June

Seeking the Holy

A woman came through the line at the door after a fabulous service of worship today, shook my hand, and asked when I was going to find a new barber. She had just spent an hour in the presence of Holy, Holy, Holy, and this was what she wanted to say to her pastor.

Parishioners don't realize that sermons rise from the deepest places of their pastor's soul, where we've been carrying around the pathos of the congregation alongside God's ideas. And when I'm in the pulpit I show up with frighteningly vulnerable transparency in order for the Word to be presented with authenticity.

It's impossible to get my soul tucked backed in before I'm standing at the door shaking hands and hearing comments about my bad haircut. Interestingly, I can't take a lot of affirmation at the door either. Mostly, I'm just hoping for, "It was great to be here today. See you next week."

I've collected a number of comments over the years that made my head cock to the side like my dog when he's confused:

"I really liked last week's sermon."

"You must not be feeling well today."

"I wish my husband could have heard that sermon."

"So you agree with the apostle Paul?"

"You know, the Episcopalians have a service that blesses dogs. Why don't we do that?"

"The pastoral prayer went six minutes today. You've got to say something to her."

But there are other comments I cannot dismiss like, "Cal is going in for surgery this Wednesday. I hope you can stop by the hospital."

As I pored over the construction of the sermon, God and I were behind closed doors wrestling for something worthy of following the opening phrase: "Hear the Word of the Lord." The director of music knocked herself out to get the right notes out of the choir in rehearsal because she knows their music is all prayer. Even the new custodian understands that something holy is going to happen in the sanctuary on Sunday morning, so he makes sure the pews are clean, the hymnbooks are in the right place, and all of the inserts from last week's bulletin have been picked up.

I've learned not to expect the congregation to be able to appreciate this sacred drama on Sunday mornings before they're ushered into a pew. Their days before Sunday were jammed up with paying bills, dealing with a teenager who screams "I hate you," the boss who's never satisfied, the broken dishwasher, and the repairman who can't get there this week. No matter how carefully we construct the liturgy, it's too much to hope they realize that this is a very different hour in their frantically reactive lives.

Ironically, all of their weekday busyness has lulled them to sleep to the point they can't possibly pay attention to the Holy in their lives. They're sleepwalking when they arrive on Sunday morning, and they may still slumber out the door after worship with no recognition of the soul-work that just occurred. It doesn't mean it didn't occur. It just means they may be prone not to notice they were just on holy ground, and so they say something dopey about my bad haircut.

Then there are those in line after worship who ask me to stop by the hospital and see their husband so I can pour a prayer over his life before surgery.

That always gives me pause and makes me think it might be the best possible response to worship. It's a way of saying, "I understand God is with us. And I needed the reminder. Thanks. But I was hoping you could say that again before they start cutting into Cal on Wednesday."

The prayer on Wednesday morning will be even more of the high drama of being in conversation with Holy, Holy, Holy that goes on all week long in my soul. I do nothing for the congregation that's more important than keeping this sacred conversation going in worship, during committee meetings, beside hospital beds, and when I'm driving home at the end of a long day.

I've never had a job description that said, "Pay attention to the holy, and then other duties as assigned." But that's actually what I try to do for the congregation. Everything else is just everything else.

Week Two

When I Can No Longer Blame Work

At our regular Starbucks conversation this afternoon Father Ted asked me, again, how I was feeling about my upcoming retirement. I know better than to give him the glib, "Well, it's about time" evasive response I toss off to most people. So I asked him, "Which feeling do you want to hear?" He sort of smiled, as if to say that was a good beginning.

I talked for a while about the easy feelings. Several years ago Ellie and I developed a bucket list of things we want to do before we die, and we're both excited to finally start checking things off the list. "No more excuses about the demands at the church. No more vacation plans interrupted by a crisis in someone's life. Now we'll regain complete control of our lives," I said with a bit of fabricated excitement.

With even less of a smile Father Ted told me I was always in control of my life. He then probed a bit by asking what I am looking forward to giving up at the church.

We went down that road for a little while. I am tired and looking forward to stepping away from the annual routines of being the pastor—gearing up for the holy days of Advent, Lent, and Easter; and the stewardship campaigns, officer retreats, strategic planning with the staff, and mission trips. Best of all, I'll be done with Youth Sundays, which I would only confess to Father Ted. And then there has been the weekly routine of staff meetings, hospital calls, committee meetings, and pastoral counseling—all while constantly preparing for the next Sunday sermon. For most of my years at the church I found comfort in these routines. But I have done it again and again, and now I am looking forward to embarking on a Monday without having a sense of how my week will go.

Father Ted shrugged and said, "Maybe it will work out that way." Then he cautioned that I could be as lost and confused as a sheepdog who wandered away from the flock.

Trying a different approach, I told my confessor that I will miss the people I've come to love and to whom I have given most of my life over all these years. Most of all, I'll miss doing the funerals of those who are going to die after I'm retired, which will probably include Mrs. Parker.

"Of course," said Father Ted. But his silence that followed was a gentle demand to dig still deeper. Sometimes it can be irritating to have a friend who's a priest.

Eventually, in exasperation I told him that I really don't have a clue how I'm going to handle this retirement. For the first time in my life, I don't know what's next. In the earlier years I was always focused on the next degree, the next job, the next rung on the ladder to climb. Then a while back I gave up all that out of my love for this congregation. I haven't updated my résumé or kept a list of my writings or achievements for a very long time. But there was still always another purposeful goal and set of challenges for the congregation. Now I'm just stepping out into a life that has no meaningful plan, and I really don't think the bucket list qualifies.

"So having a plan is what has always been important to you?" he asked me.

I started to backpedal and said a bunch of stuff about how this will be God's new creative edge in my life. It will be good to learn how to sacrifice my need for a plan, I claimed.

Expecting to be affirmed for this spiritual statement, all I got was another "Maybe."

This time I pressed Father Ted: "What do you mean, 'Maybe'?"

He said that it may be that God created me as a planner, and not just to help my career or the congregation. "You Presbyterians have so much self-loathing for your work ethic and your organizational affections. You know it isn't inherently spiritual to be spontaneous. Even God has plans. I hope."

He is right, of course. Protestants have been riding on the Catholic contemplative tradition for a long time. The best part of that impulse comes from our ecumenical commitment to embrace all of the Christian faith. But it's also true that we keep trying to run away from all of our strategic planning and work ethic because it leaves us tired. And we assume that means we're doing something harmful to our souls. My hunch is that most of the Bible's heroes were often tired, beat up, and confused. But every morning they returned to the best plan they had.

Then Father Ted gave up the "Maybe" stuff and came in for the kill. "You're anxious because you don't have a meaningful retirement plan. So get a plan. And stop thinking that you now have to become someone else. God would never ask that of you. And don't you dare think of that as being spiritual."

His point was pretty convicting—this retirement is my opportunity to embrace the self I have always been but can no longer blame on my work. As he said, I was always in control of myself even when I didn't want to admit it.

Trying to wrap up this hard conversation, I told Father Ted that was a pretty good sermon for a Catholic. He swiped away my teasing and asked, "So what have you decided about telling the congregation that you have cancer?"

Still Holding Back Part of Me

I will be leaving the church very soon. There's been a lot of congregational focus on the retirement party, the last worship service, the last meeting with the elders, the last staff meeting, the last . . . This is starting to remind me of Joe Lincoln's embarrassment at not dying after saying goodbye to all of his loved ones.

As far as I know the congregation still doesn't know about my cancer. At least I haven't told them. It's not that I decided not to. Apparently, I've decided to not decide. At our last conversation Father Ted asked again if I was planning on saying anything to the congregation about the disease. I don't think he's advocating for a choice one way or the other. But I know he was gently accusing me of not dealing with the question of whether or not I'll disclose this. Ellie's been doing the same thing, but mostly because it means she can't talk or pray with any of her friends in the church about this until I decide. I feel bad that my reluctance has come at a cost to her.

It is now clear that I won't be saying anything to the church about this disease. Not when I am soon leaving them. It wouldn't be fair to drop that emotional bomb into the middle of the congregation and then tack on, "But you won't be able to express concern for me because I'm moving away." I don't know when exactly it was, but I have clearly passed the fail-safe point of responsibly disclosing this disease. The diagnosis came last November, but I've held it so closely for so long that it has to remain part of the me that I cannot give to the congregation.

Why did I handle it like this? It's not my nature to back my way into a situation where the choices were made for me. But that's exactly what happened here. Something was going on beneath the surface to compel me to let time make the decision. It is odd that I would be so transparent about my many mistakes and failures, most of which have shown up in sermon illustrations, but I could never make the conscious choice to reveal a current medical problem.

At first, I wondered if it was because I was afraid of appearing vulnerable to the congregation. But now I doubt that, because they're aware of worse things about me than being sick. Was it because I was in denial of the disease and making it public would only make it more real? But the doctors, lab technicians, and radiation treatments have all convinced me that this disease is very real. For a while I was thinking that I didn't tell the congregation about it for the same reason I wouldn't tell them about having a root canal. This isn't deadly; it's just a hassle. Lots of people had this disease and are walking around just fine today. But if I thought it was no big deal I would have surely used it as a sermon illustration.

Here's what I'm thinking these days: as much as I love this congregation, I don't want to give them everything about my life. As long as I can hold something back, there is still a part of me that exists beyond the grasping reach of the congregation. It's my disease that I will treat with my doctors, and I will find comfort only in my family and close friends who are not part of the church. I can't love the church if I give them everything about me, or there won't be a me to give. As hard as it is on my flamingly extroverted wife not to talk about this with her friends in the church, she too understands this is my way of hanging on to me and even us. This has always been true, and something deep in me needs to keep it that way through the end of this ministry.

The Last Surprise

Last night was my big-bash retirement party. It was everything Ellie and I were afraid it would be. And yet we loved it. The hotel ballroom was packed with members of the congregation, other pastors, and our friends in the community. Even the mayor dropped by for a bit. The planning committee had secretly invited Mackenzie and her family, who surprised us by flying in for the event, which kept Ellie in tears most of the night.

Rather than the loud band I feared they would hire, they also surprised us with some of the guys from my college a cappella group. I still have no idea how they tracked them down. My hope of having the director of music lead us in a hymn or two in the church fellowship hall took a funny turn into me joining my old friends in singing "Under the Boardwalk."

The program included several testimonials that were almost a roast. Mrs. Parker's son told the crowd that his mother would love to have been there if only she could remember who I was. Grumpy old Alice Matthews said she knew she would outlast me at the church. Father Ted told everyone I owed him thousands of dollars in therapy fees. And I'm trying not to remember the stories the guys from college told.

There wasn't anything overtly religious about the evening. I'm trying to remember if anyone even prayed at any point in the night. But there certainly was an awful lot of laughter. As we drove home my wife and I couldn't stop talking about how surprising the evening was, and most of all how surprised we were that we enjoyed this ending to our days at the congregation.

Everything about me, everything I have done in this congregation over the many years, led me to expect we would wrap up my pastoral ministry the same way we worshiped, fellowshipped, and expressed deep care for each other over all these years. That's why I was pushing for the low-key event at the church where we would say tender things to each other. But the congregation believed there had been plenty of informal ways of doing that since I announced my retirement, and they really didn't want me to be pastoral last night. They just wanted to laugh with me.

I am pretty certain that the planning committee never had a secret meeting in executive session when they decided that it would be best to use this retirement party to demonstrate that my pastoral relationship with them had come to an end, and that's why we couldn't do what we've always done together in the church. But to use Father Ted's word, "maybe" they had an intuitive sense of that. Maybe they were setting me free. And maybe that was a more profound "I love you."

I now realize that if last night had gone as I'd planned, I would still have been functioning as the pastor, and probably would have needed to follow up the evening with more pastoral care. But the congregation knew better. What we needed was to laugh, tease, and spend an evening not being at all churchy.

Laughter is a grace that cannot be planned because it's never expected. The pastor who was trying to carefully plan a tearful goodbye has a rowdy party instead. And he loves it, because it means those he thought he would have to tear from his breast were actually telling him to take off the collar and lighten up. What else could I do but laugh?

The book of Revelation ends with God being at home among mortals. And there is a River of Life, and from the river grows a tree with leaves for the healing of the nations. It's a beautiful ending to the story for which the church has strived for thousands of years to find some approximation. But when I read the *New York Times* every morning, that vision seems laughable. Right. That's exactly right. That's how the unexpected ending is supposed to go. There's a very thin line between laughter and praise.

Of course, in spite of all of the worldwide church's best efforts, and in spite of all its worst ones, only God can give us this glorious ending on earth. It's going to be sheer grace, as it's been all along.

Certainly everything good that has unfolded during my tenure at this congregation has come by God's grace. No one is clearer about that than I am. And the best response to grace is praise, gratitude, joy, and maybe even a bit of laughter at a pastor who was trying too hard.

Today I find myself wondering how the leaders of the congregation knew a party was what we all needed. What I fear is the dark voice that claims they were whooping it up that I finally got a clue it was time to go. But I know better. This has never been an easy congregation, but it has been a loving one. If they thought I was outstaying my welcome, they would have told me. And each other. But there was never a whiff of that.

What I know is that people don't laugh when they are afraid or anxious. Maybe the decision to throw a party meant that the church was healthy enough for me to leave. If that is true, it can only be because they have faith in God's faithfulness.

What I want to believe is that they knew my departure from our loving community was as hard on me as it was on them. So they decided to give me the most extraordinary retirement gift of all: a benediction. "We're okay. There will be another pastor. You can go in peace."

Epilogue

It has been a few months since I finished writing this diary on my last year of being a pastor. After reading it several times, I find it striking that while digging around in the subtext of my parishioners' lives, I was so oblivious to my own anxieties about retirement. It wasn't that I was in denial of my decision to stop being the pastor; I just didn't do much internal work to prepare for it.

Father Ted kept telling me to get a plan. I actually had lots of plans—financial plans, relocation plans, plans for the congregation, even plans for the retirement party. But I didn't really plan on not being the pastor of St. Andrews. If I wanted to get myself off the hook for that failure, I could say that I just wanted to deeply enter every day of my last year. And if I wanted to be self-critical, I could say that I never saw how deeply enmeshed I was in my work. My hunch is that both of those dynamics are true. It is also true that my soul, which had so long been crowded by parishioners, had no idea how to plan to go it alone.

Like all of the times I have clung to something, fearing I would fall into the abyss by letting go, I find that in retirement I'm falling only into mystery.

I already miss the routines of my work at St. Andrews, which I once thought would be a relief to leave behind. I miss walking into the Gothic building every morning and sensing the sturdiness of the church's stones before I had to confront a single decision. I miss the moments when I felt overwhelmed by the pathos of ministry and would wander into the sanctuary where it was empty, dark, lonely, and the perfect place for prayer. And I miss the congregation. I feel like a missionary who spent his life among the people he came to love but eventually had to sail back to a home he's never known before.

I have a long way to go before I can say I have figured out this chapter of my internal life. But at least one thing has become clear in my thinking over the last few months. There is no theology of retirement. It's a modern invention that creates a horizontal organization to life as if it has a beginning, middle, and end. Retirement has become a way of trying to enjoy some days without purpose before we get to the end. But that has never been what our faith claimed about our stewardship of life. We're created to live each day under heaven as an eternal gift filled with more grace and wonder than we know how to receive or could ever see.

Our calling is to live vertically, under the God who broke into our humanity in Christ and who through the Spirit is still doing that every day. Eternity isn't out there in the future, or even up there, somewhere. It's here. The Almighty God of Heaven and Earth is with us. So I haven't actually been moving toward the end and then whatever comes after that. I've always been living under the eternal mystery of whatever may come today.

I have actually always believed this, but I got too distracted to enjoy it. There was always one more sermon to prepare, one more strategic plan filled with new programs, one more pastoral counseling session—all focused on proclaiming *God is with us*—so that I never gave myself the opportunity to think much about God being with me apart from my petitions as a pastor. Now that

I'm not busy talking about eternal mystery, I have to attend to my own mysterious life. My fear is that I'll find it pretty boring. Other people's lives have always fascinated me, but I no longer have their cover when I'm talking to God.

The move from our house in town to the cabin by the lake was another distraction of busyness for over a month. But we're very much here now. I love its constant smell of pine, the way the lake is always changing colors, our wood-rimmed canoe, and the various places I find Ellie's fishing poles lying around. Since it has long been our vacation home, it wasn't like we were moving to a strange place. That meant we could focus more on the strangeness of our life in a place not invaded by my work.

I've set up another Study in one of the guest bedrooms. I gave away about half of my books, but there's still plenty to surround the Italian desk I kept for the journey to the new home. I still go to The Study to read, write articles that may or may not get published, email Father Ted and James Kairns, handwrite letters to Mackenzie, and prepare sermons for the occasional guest preaching opportunities that come my way—which Ellie calls Rent-a-Reverend gigs. There's always work to do, but now that I don't have a job, I realize more clearly that I'm working simply because I've always enjoyed it.

On most Sundays we worship at the small Episcopal church near the lake. It has taken me a while to get used to the liturgy, which has so many words, but I love kneeling to receive the body of Christ from a priest. I thought I would chafe against going to church without getting paid for it, but kneeling at the rail is often the highlight of my week. It's going to take a long time to get used to the view from the pews. My chair used to be turned toward the congregation so that I could remember the words I had collected from them before going to the pulpit to say "Hear the Word of the Lord." Now I only see the altar and the young priest who doesn't know me, and the truly awful choir. I know that should be good enough.

Mrs. Parker, my favorite elder whom I dearly love, died last week. Ellie and I will drive down to attend the funeral, but the interim pastor will conduct the service. That's how it is supposed to work in our church tradition, but I have no idea how I'll handle the sadness of sitting in the pew for her funeral.

The treatments for the cancer have come to an end. There were a few more long rides back to the town where we used to live in order to wrap up the radiation therapy. A month ago, the doctors said I had just as good a chance of getting hit by a bus as being done in by this disease. Fortunately, there is no bus service at the lake. But I'm able to focus a bit more now on what it meant that this scare came along during my last year of work when I was so focused on being the pastor to others. Some of that is obvious, but I suspect there are deeper insights that will take a lot more time to figure out.

Ellie and I are figuring out our rhythms of life together without St. Andrews between us. She has become my new old lover. We're a bit tentative with each other these days, which feels strange emotionally but makes sense when we talk about it. She's always wanted more of my time, and we both blamed the job for the lack of it. Even my need for time in The Study was always understood as a demand of the job. It's probably always been clear to Ellie, but it's now painfully clear to me that I just need time alone to breathe. It's the same language I once used to describe the August vacations from work, and how I made excuses for my routine of going to The Study after dinner. There can be no more churchy excuses or cover for that need for a blessed place of quiet sanctuary. It's clear now that it's always been just me being me.

Yet even as I write this in The Study, I don't want to stay here long. I miss her when I spend too much time with my books or on another writing project. Even while I'm in here, I need to know that she's around working in the kitchen or on the Mustang that moved with us to the cabin, running errands, talking to a client whose living room she's overhauling, or chasing down her friends on Facebook. When she goes away to help Mackenzie with a project or to visit one of her siblings without me, I miss her terribly. We've begun a practice of taking long walks every morning, which we conclude by stopping by the coffeehouse. Along the way we talk about the family, the things we're working on, what we read in the *New York Times*, and what we'll make for dinner. Then we get home and spend time with our different projects. But I find I don't have the old sense of devotion to them I once had, and Ellie never did.

The devotion these days is simply to these days.